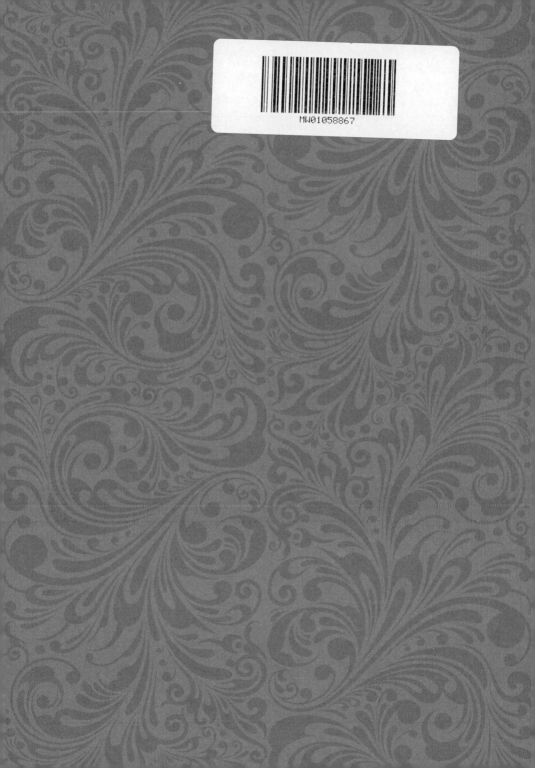

Presented to

....

From

From

Date

Spiritual Refreshment *for* Women

Morning & Evening

BARBOUR BOOKS

An Imprint of Barbour Publishing, Inc.

© 2015 by Barbour Publishing, Inc.

Print ISBN 978-1-63409-220-3

eBook Editions:
Adobe Digital Edition (.epub) 978-1-63409-549-5
Kindle and MobiPocket Edition (.prc) 978-1-63409-550-1

Devotional thoughts from *Everyday Love, Everyday Joy, Everyday Wisdom, Everyday Hope* and *Everyday Grace* published by Barbour Publishing, Inc.

Scripture quotations marked NASB are taken from the New American Standard Bible, © 1960, 1962, 1963, 1968, 1971, 1972, 1973, 1975, 1977, 1995 by The Lockman Foundation. Used by permission.

Scripture quotations marked KJV are taken from the King James Version of the Bible.

Scripture quotations marked NKJV are taken from the New King James Version®. Copyright © 1982 by Thomas Nelson, Inc. Used by permission. All rights reserved.

Scripture quotations marked NRSV are taken from the New Revised Standard Version Bible, copyright 1989, Division of Christian Education of the National Council of the Churches of Christ in the United States of America. Used by permission. All rights reserved.

Scripture quotations marked TLB are taken from The Living Bible © 1971 by Tyndale House Foundation. Used by permission of Tyndale House Publishers, Inc. Wheaton, Illinois 60189. All rights reserved.

Scripture quotations marked NIV are taken from the HOLY BIBLE, NEW INTERNATIONAL VERSION®. NIV®. Copyright © 1973, 1978, 1984, 2011 by Biblica, Inc.™ Used by permission. All rights reserved worldwide.

Scripture quotations marked MSG are from THE MESSAGE. Copyright © by Eugene H. Peterson 1993, 1994, 1995, 1996, 2000, 2001, 2002. Used by permission of NavPress Publishing Group.

Scripture quotations marked ESV are from The Holy Bible, English Standard Version®, copyright © 2001 by Crossway Bibles, a publishing ministry of Good News Publishers. Used by permission. All rights reserved.

Scripture quotations marked NLT are taken from the *Holy Bible*. New Living Translation copyright© 1996, 2004, 2007 by Tyndale House Foundation. Used by permission of Tyndale House Publishers, Inc. Carol Stream, Illinois 60188. All rights reserved.

Scripture quotations marked NCV are taken from the New Century Version of the Bible, copyright © 2005 by Thomas Nelson, Inc. Used by permission. All rights reserved.

Scripture quotations marked CEV are from the Contemporary English Version, Copyright © 1995 by American Bible Society. Used by permission.

Scripture quotations marked TNIV are taken from the Holy Bible, Today's New International Version®. Copyright © 2001, 2005 by Biblica®. Used by permission of Biblica®. All rights reserved worldwide.

Scripture quotations marked HCSB are taken from the Holman Christian Standard Bible ® Copyright © 1999, 2000, 2002, 2003, 2009 by Holman Bible Publishers. Used by permission.

Published by Barbour Books, an imprint of Barbour Publishing, Inc., P.O. Box 719, Uhrichsville, Ohio 44683, www.barbourbooks.com

Our mission is to publish and distribute inspirational products offering exceptional value and biblical encouragement to the masses.

 Member of the
Evangelical Christian
Publishers Association

Printed in China.

Morning and Evening
Wisdom for Your Soul

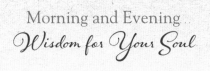

Evening, and morning. . .
will I pray, and cry aloud:
and he shall hear my voice.

PSALM 55:17 KJV

This lovely *Spiritual Refreshment for Women: Morning and Evening
Edition* will help you experience an intimate connection to the
heavenly Father with a brief devotional thought and scripture—
twice a day for every day of the year. Enhance your spiritual journey
with the refreshing readings and come to know just how
deeply and tenderly God loves you.
Be blessed!

Morning
Know My Heart

Search me, O God, and know my heart;
test me and know my anxious thoughts.
PSALM 139:23 NLT

Have you ever asked the Lord to give you an "anxiety check"? He longs for you to live in peace, but that won't happen as long as you're driven by worries and fears. Today, allow Him to search your heart. Ask Him to dig deep. Are there cobwebs that need to be swept out? Things hidden that should be revealed? Let God wash away your anxieties, replacing them with His exceeding great joy!

Evening
His Love toward Us

For great is his love toward us, and the faithfulness
of the LORD endures forever. Praise the LORD.
PSALM 117:2 NIV

We'll never be able to understand God's love toward us. It extends grace when grace is the last thing we deserve. It offers forgiveness when we've committed the most heinous of sins. It reaches out to us when we're haughty and proud and comes looking for us when we've sunk to the lowest low. Doesn't that kind of love make you feel like shouting? Like praising God at the top of your voice?

MORNING
Attitude Equals Outcome

Serve the LORD with gladness:
come before his presence with singing.
PSALM 100:2 KJV

Attitude is everything. Our attitude determines our outcome.
We are challenged by scripture to serve with gladness. (It's funny to
think of *service* and *gladness* in the same sentence, isn't it?) But here's
the truth: If we serve with an attitude of joy, it changes everything.
Our service doesn't feel like service anymore. It's a privilege!

EVENING
Enter into the Joy

His lord said unto him, Well done, thou good and faithful servant:
thou hast been faithful over a few things, I will make thee ruler
over many things: enter thou into the joy of thy lord.
MATTHEW 25:21 KJV

When you think of standing before the Lord face-to-face are you
overwhelmed with fear or awestruck with great joy? Oh, what a glorious
day it will be, when we hear Him speak those words, "Well done,
thou good and faithful servant." When He ushers us into the joy of
His presence for all eternity, our fears and hesitations will be
forever washed away. Spend time in joyous rehearsal today!

MORNING
Anxiety is a Joy Killer

Be anxious for nothing, but in everything by prayer and supplication
with thanksgiving let your requests be made known to God.
PHILIPPIANS 4:6 NASB

Be anxious for nothing? Is that possible? Aren't my anxieties
tied to my emotions? And aren't my emotions tied to the things
that happen to me? I can't control what happens to me, so how can
I control my reactions? Deep breath, friend! Instead of knee-jerking
when troubles come, slip into the throne room and spend some
time giving those problems to the Lord. With thanksgiving,
let your requests be made known to Him.

EVENING
The Bigger Picture

"But you, be strong and do not lose courage,
for there is reward for your work."
2 CHRONICLES 15:7 NASB

Why do you work? For a paycheck? For respect? For a sense of
self-worth? All of those things are good reasons to work, but never
forget that your work is part of a bigger picture. God wants to use
your hands, your intelligence, and your efforts to build His
kingdom, the place where grace dwells.

MORNING
The Fruit of Your Labor

You will eat the fruit of your labor;
blessings and prosperity will be yours.
PSALM 128:2 NIV

We're always waiting for the payoff, aren't we? When we've
put a lot of effort into a project, for example, we hope to see good
results. The Word of God promises that we will eat the fruit of
our labor that we will eventually experience blessings and prosperity.
So, all of that hard work will be worth it. But remember,
the joy is in the journey! It's not just in the payoff.

EVENING
I Will Bow Down

I will bow down toward your holy temple and will praise
your name for your unfailing love and your faithfulness, for you have
so exalted your solemn decree that it surpasses your fame.
PSALM 138:2 NIV

Sometimes we come into God's presence and we feel like shouting
for joy. At other times His love drives us to our knees. Oh, how we're
humbled by what He has done for us. We kneel in His presence and
praise His name, not just for His gifts, but also for His moment-by-
moment offering of love. Our God is worthy to be praised!

Morning
No Boundaries!

For as high as the heavens are above the earth, so great is
his love for those who fear him; as far as the east is from the west,
so far has he removed our transgressions from us.
PSALM 103:11–12 NIV

God's love for us surpasses all boundaries. If we go to the highest highs or the lowest lows, He will meet us there. No matter where we are in our faith journey, He stands with arms wide, ready to forgive our sins. We don't understand this kind of love. Then again, if we could understand it, perhaps it wouldn't feel like such a gift. Thank God for a love that knows no boundaries.

Evening
Good Enough

Leah's eyes were weak, but Rachel was beautiful of form and face.
GENESIS 29:17 NASB

Have you ever felt like a booby prize? No doubt Leah did. Hunky Jacob labored seven years to marry Leah's gorgeous sister, Rachel. Then their squirrelly father switched his daughters at the altar. Jacob freaked. Leah tanked. We, too, sometimes feel that we're not good enough; that we don't measure up. But Leah gave birth to six of the twelve tribes of Israel, the cornerstone of Judeo-Christendom. God has a mighty plan for all of us Leahs.

MORNING
Ever Wider

A longing fulfilled is a tree of life.
PROVERBS 13:12 NIV

Take stock of your life. What were you most hoping to achieve a year ago? (Or five years ago?) How many of those goals have been achieved? Sometimes, once we've reached a goal, we move on too quickly to the next one, never allowing ourselves to find the grace God wants to reveal within that achievement. With each goal reached, His grace spreads out into your life, like a tree whose branches grow ever wider.

EVENING
The Joy of Heaven

I saw the LORD sitting upon his throne, and all the host of heaven standing on his right hand and on his left.
2 CHRONICLES 18:18 KJV

What do you think of when you ponder the word *heaven*? What will it be like to walk on streets of gold, to see our loved ones who have gone before us? How thrilling, to know we will one day meet our Lord and Savior face-to-face. He has gone to prepare a place for us—and what a place it will be! The joy of eternity is ours as believers. Praise Him!

MORNING

Abiding Love

Whoever confesses that Jesus is the Son of God,
God abides in him, and he in God. So we have
come to know and to believe the love that God has
for us. God is love, and whoever abides in love
abides in God, and God abides in him.

1 JOHN 4:15–16 ESV

Are you wowed by God's unending love? It's pretty amazing, isn't it? Once we discover it—and see that it has no limits—we are awed by such spectacular love! All we have to do to receive this love is confess that Jesus is the Son of God. When we do, the Creator of heaven and earth sweeps in and abides in us. Praise the Lord for His abiding love!

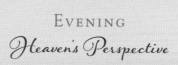

EVENING

Heaven's Perspective

Always give yourselves fully to the work of the Lord,
because you know that your labor in the Lord is not in vain.

1 CORINTHIANS 15:58 NIV

You may feel sometimes as though all of your hard work comes to nothing. But if your work is the Lord's work, you can trust Him to bring it to fulfillment. You may not always know what is being accomplished in the light of eternity, but God knows. And when you look back from heaven's perspective, you will be able to see how much grace was accomplished through all of your hard work.

MORNING
Too Wonderful to Be Measured

I want you to know all about Christ's love,
although it is too wonderful to be measured.
Then your lives will be filled with all that God is.
EPHESIANS 3:19 CEV

Have you ever thought about measuring God's love? There's no ruler long enough! No map wide enough. No ocean deep enough. God's love is immeasurable. It is, as we sang as children, deep and wide. If we spent our lives trying to make sense of it, it would only outrun us in the end.

EVENING
Rejoice in His Love!

I will be glad and rejoice in your love, for you saw
my affliction and knew the anguish of my soul.
PSALM 31:7 NIV

Are you one of those people who loves to praise God? Do you enjoy lifting your heart and voice to Him in glorious song for all He's done? The Lord loves it when His children offer a sacrifice of praise. And why not? His love provokes us to exalt Him. When we think about it, when we come to fully understand it, how can we do anything but praise?

Morning
A Solid Foundation

A bad motive can't achieve a good end.
PROVERBS 17:20 MSG

We hear it all the time: the end justifies the means. But that is not how it works in the kingdom of God. It's like trying to build a beautiful house on a shaky foundation. It just doesn't work. Sooner or later, the weak foundation will affect the rest of the house. True achievement is built on God's grace and love. That is the kind of foundation that holds solid no matter what.

Evening
Granter of Dreams

Hope deferred makes the heart sick,
but a dream fulfilled is a tree of life.
PROVERBS 13:12 NLT

As a teenager, I dreamed of one day writing a book. But life intervened, and I became a wife, mother, occupational therapist, and piano teacher. My writing dream was shelved. Twenty-five years later, after my youngest chick flew the coop, God's still, small voice whispered, "It's time." Within five years, the Granter of Dreams delivered over seventy articles and nine book contracts.
What's your dream? Be brave and take the first step.

MORNING
Perfection

I don't mean to say that I have already achieved these things or that I have already reached perfection. But I press on to possess that perfection for which Christ Jesus first possessed me.
PHILIPPIANS 3:12 NLT

We are called to be perfect. Nothing else is good enough for God's people. That doesn't mean we have an inflated sense of our own worth. And it doesn't mean we beat ourselves up when we fall short of perfection. We know that in our own strength we can never hope to achieve perfection—but with God's grace, anything is possible.

EVENING
The Promise of Eternal Life

And this is what he promised us—eternal life.
1 JOHN 2:25 NIV

Ever had a friend or loved one make a promise, only to break it? What about you? Ever broken a promise? We all fail in this area, don't we? Thankfully, God is not a promise breaker. When He promised you would spend eternity with Him if you accepted the work of His Son on the cross. . .He meant it. Doesn't it bring joy to your heart to know God won't break His promises?

MORNING
For God So Loved. . .

For God so loved the world, that he gave his only begotten Son,
that whosoever believeth in him should not perish, but have everlasting life.
JOHN 3:16 KJV

If we spent the rest of our lives trying to figure out the heart of God for His people, we couldn't do it. What kind of father gives his son as a sacrifice for the lives of countless billions of people? And all He asks in response is that we believe so that we can receive His immeasurable gift of love. Today open your heart to believe—and receive!

EVENING
Control

Put GOD in charge of your work,
then what you've planned will take place
PROVERBS 16:3 MSG

If we're doing a job that is important to us, it is hard to let go of our control. Not only do we hate to trust someone else to take over, but we often don't want to trust God to take charge either. We want to do it all by ourselves. But the best laid plans fall into nothing without God's help. What's more, as we rely on His grace, we no longer need to feel stressed or pressured! We can let Him take charge.

MORNING
Filled with Joy

And the disciples were filled with joy,
and with the Holy Ghost.

ACTS 13:52 KJV

Want to know the secret of walking in the fullness of joy? Draw near to the Lord. Allow His Spirit to fill you daily. Let Him whisper sweet nothings in your ear and woo you with His love. The Spirit of God is your Comforter, your Friend. He fills you to overflowing. Watch the joy flow!

EVENING
Give Thanks to the Lord

After consulting the people, Jehoshaphat appointed men to sing to the LORD and to praise him for the splendor of his holiness as they went out at the head of the army, saying: "Give thanks to the LORD, for his love endures forever."

2 CHRONICLES 20:21 NIV

Don't you love early mornings? They're filled with promise. New day. New dawn. New chance to experience God's awesome love. He is pleased when we make a choice to give thanks early in the day. His enduring love never sleeps, so it meets us fresh every morning. Praise Him for that unfailing love, even before your eyes are fully open!

MORNING
Laying Down Your Life

"Greater love has no one than this:
to lay down one's life for one's friends."
JOHN 15:13 NIV

Have you ever wondered if you would be willing—or able—
to lay down your life for someone else (say, a family member, child,
or spouse)? Could you do it? Very few human beings have literally
laid down their lives. However, Jesus, who lived a sinless life,
willingly gave Himself as a sacrifice for us, His friends. He laid down
His life so that we can have life eternal. Oh, what love!

EVENING
Stop the Roller Coaster

Why am I discouraged? Why is my heart so sad? I will put my hope in God!
I will praise him again—my Savior and my God!
PSALM 43:5 NLT

For women, ruts of depression are often caused by careening hormones.
Rampaging hormones can cause us to spend countless hours weeping
without knowing why–or bite someone's head off, lose precious sleep,
or sprout funky nervous habits. Knowing that this hormonally-crazed
state is only temporary, we must intentionally place our hope in
tomorrow and pray that God will turn the downside up!

MORNING
Joy. . .Minute by Minute

Keep your eyes focused on what is right,
and look straight ahead to what is good.
PROVERBS 4:25 NCV

Ever wonder how you can be perfectly happy one minute and upset the
next? If joy is a choice, then it's one you have to make. . .continually.
We are often ruled by our emotions, which is why it's so important
to stay focused, especially when you're having a tough day. Don't let
frustration steal even sixty seconds from you. Instead, choose joy!

EVENING
Freedom in Forgiveness

"If you forgive the sins of any, their sins have been forgiven them;
if you retain the sins of any, they have been retained."
JOHN 20:23 NASB

Ever known someone who simply refused to forgive? It's one thing
to cling to past hurts because you're unable to let go; it's another
to do so out of spite. There are no stipulations on forgiveness.
We must forgive, regardless of what has been done to us. If you are
struggling to release someone who's hurt you, ask the Lord to help you.
A miracle of joy will take place as you release your grip.

MORNING
His Great Love

But God showed his great love for us by sending
Christ to die for us while we were still sinners.
ROMANS 5:8 NLT

Have you ever tried to think up ways to show others that you love them? Maybe you send roses or write a great letter. Perhaps you go out of your way to do something sacrificial so that they will recognize your great love. God went out of His way to show us how much He loves us by offering His only Son. What an amazing example of how to love!

EVENING
Secret Places

What you're after is
truth from the inside out.
PSALM 51:6 MSG

Sometimes we are like Adam and Eve in the garden after they had sinned; we are afraid to come naked into God's presence. We think we can hide ourselves from Him. But God cannot teach our hearts if we refuse to be open with Him. We must take the risk of stepping into His presence with complete honesty and vulnerability. When we do, His grace touches us at our deepest, most secret places, and we are filled with His wisdom.

MORNING
Lifting the Spirit of Heaviness

Anxiety weighs down the heart,
but a kind word cheers it up.
PROVERBS 12:25 NIV

Want to know how to get beyond a season of heaviness? Want to enter a season of joy? Speak uplifting, positive words. The things that come out of your mouth can make or break you. After all, we tend to believe what we hear. So, let words of joy flow. Speak hope. Speak life. And watch that spirit of heaviness take flight!

EVENING
Sing for Joy

But let all who take refuge in you be glad; let them ever sing for joy.
Spread your protection over them, that those who
love your name may rejoice in you.
PSALM 5:11 NIV

There are so many things to rejoice over when you're in love with the Creator of heaven and earth, and rejoicing changes your perspective on everything! Remember that little song you used to sing as a child: "I've got the joy, joy, joy, joy down in my heart!" It's true. Love gives birth to joy. And when that joy spills over, watch out! It's contagious!

MORNING
A Fruit Tree

But the fruit of the Spirit is love, joy, peace, forbearance, kindness, goodness, faithfulness, gentleness and self-control. Against such things there is no law.
GALATIANS 5:22–23 NIV

If love were a tree, it would be heavy with fruit. What fruit, you ask? Oh, many varieties! When you love people, you're naturally more patient with them. And you treat them kindly and use self-control. You're faithful to those you love, and you respond in a gentle fashion. These things are the "fruit" of a love relationship that comes from on high.

EVENING
A Little Goes a Long Way

The LORD our God has allowed a few of us to survive as a remnant.
EZRA 9:8 NLT

Remnants. Useless by most standards, aren't they? But God is in the business of using tiny slivers of what's left to do mighty things. In the passage above, Nehemiah rebuilt the fallen walls of Jerusalem with a remnant of Israel; Noah's three sons repopulated the earth after the flood; four slave boys—Daniel, Shadrach, Meshach, and Abednego— kept faith alive for an entire nation. When it feels as if bits and pieces are all that has survived of your hope, remember how *much* God can accomplish with remnants!

MORNING
Shifting Sands

Let us hold unswervingly to the hope we profess,
for he who promised is faithful.
HEBREWS 10:23 NIV

Change usually shakes us to the core. However, if you've been in a season of great suffering and you sense change is coming. . .you have reason to celebrate! The sands are shifting. The mourning is coming to an end. God, in His remarkable way, is reaching down with His fingertip and writing, "Look forward to tomorrow!" in the sand. Let the joy of that promise dwell in your heart. . .and bring you peace.

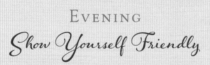

EVENING
Show Yourself Friendly

A man that hath friends must shew himself friendly:
and there is a friend that sticketh closer than a brother.
PROVERBS 18:24 KJV

Ever met someone who just seems to have the gift of friendship? She's a joy to be around and is always there when you need her. Perhaps you're that kind of friend to others. Friendship is a privilege, and we're blessed to have brothers and sisters in Christ. But not all friendships are easy. Today, ask the Lord to show you how to "show yourself friendly" in every situation. Oh, the joy of great relationships!

MORNING

Steady. . .

People with their minds set on you, you keep completely whole,
Steady on their feet, because they keep at it and don't quit.
ISAIAH 26:3 MSG

One of the meanings of *grace* is "an effortless beauty of movement."
A person with this kind of grace doesn't trip over her own feet; she's
not clumsy or awkward, but instead she moves easily, fluidly, steadily.
From a spiritual perspective, most of us stumble quite a bit—and yet
we don't give up. We know that God holds our hands, and He will
keep us steady even when we would otherwise fall flat on our faces.

EVENING

Walkin' Boots

I heard about you from others;
now I have seen you with my own eyes.
JOB 42:5 CEV

As children we sang, "Jesus loves me, this I know; for the Bible
tells me so," and we believed because, well, we were told to.
But we reach a crossroads as adults: either pull on the boots of
faith and take ownership or simply polish them occasionally—
maybe at Easter and Christmas—and allow them to sit neglected
and dusty in the closet. Have you taken ownership of your faith?
Go ahead, sister, those boots were made for walkin'!

MORNING
An Offering of Joy

Then my head will be exalted above the enemies who surround me;
at his sacred tent I will sacrifice with shouts of joy;
I will sing and make music to the LORD.
PSALM 27:6 NIV

It's one thing to offer a sacrifice of joy when things are going your way and people are treating you fairly. But when you've been through a terrible betrayal, it's often hard to recapture that feeling of joy. As you face hurts and betrayals, remember that God is the lifter of your head. Sing praises and continue to offer a sacrifice of joy!

EVENING
Those Who Love Salvation

But may all who seek you rejoice and be glad in you; may those
who love your salvation always say, "The LORD be exalted!"
PSALM 40:16 NIV

When you think about what Jesus did on the cross for you, how does it make you feel? Overwhelmed? Grateful? Filled with joy? The free gift of salvation gives us all the reason we could ever need to lift our voices in praise to God. There on Calvary, He poured out His love for humankind. And now we have the glorious privilege of pouring out our praise in response.

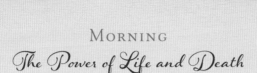

Morning
The Power of Life and Death

The tongue has the power of life and death,
and those who love it will eat its fruit.
PROVERBS 18:21 NIV

Have you ever been around people who have a sharp tongue? They don't come across as loving, do they? No, they convey just the opposite. The Bible tells us that the power of life and death is found in the tongue. When we speak words of love, we bring life. When we offer sharp retorts and ugly criticism, we imply that our love has limitations. Today make a choice to spread life. Spread love!

Evening
Stinkin' Thinkin'

Let us be sober, having put on the breastplate of faith and love,
and as a helmet, the hope of salvation.
1 THESSALONIANS 5:8 NASB

Women's hats aren't as popular as they once were, but you wouldn't know it by my closet. I love accessorizing with a perky hat to make a statement, to disguise a bad hair day, or to keep my brain from sautéing in the sizzling Florida sun. The Bible says we need to protect our minds from bad spiritual rays, too. Nasty input produces nasty output: stinkin' thinkin'. When we're tempted to input a questionable movie or book, let's don our salvation helmets and say, "No way!"

MORNING
Christ-Balance

Jesus caught them off balance with his own test question:
"What do you think about the Christ? Whose son is he?"
MATTHEW 22:41 MSG

Sometimes Christ asks us to find new ways of thinking. . .new ways
of living. . .new ways of encountering Him in the world around us.
That is not always easy. We don't like to be caught off balance.
When our life's equilibrium is shaken, we feel anxious,
out of control. But if we rely on Christ, He will pick us up,
dust us off, and give us the grace to find our balance in Him.

EVENING
A Joyous Treasure

"I enjoyed your friendship so much.
Your love to me was wonderful."
2 SAMUEL 1:26 NCV

Imagine finding a trunk in your attic. You've never noticed it before.
It's locked, but you manage to pry it open. Inside, to your great
amazement, you find gold and silver coins. Hundreds of them! That
treasure is no more special no more amazing than finding a friend.
When you find a "kindred spirit" you've discovered a priceless treasure.
Oh, the joy of a godly friendship!

MORNING

Only Joy Remains

*These things have I spoken unto you, that my joy
might remain in you, and that your joy might be full.*
JOHN 15:11 KJV

When you've been badly hurt, it's hard to let go of the pain,
isn't it? Sometimes it can crowd out everything your peace of mind,
your enthusiasm, your joy. If you're struggling with the effects of a
betrayal today, don't allow it to consume you. Release it to God.
Ask Him to replace the pain with His joy, a joy that will remain
in you, never to be stolen again.

EVENING

Inexplicable Strength

The joy of the LORD is your strength.
NEHEMIAH 8:10 NASB

Joy is not based on the circumstances around us. It is not synonymous
with happiness. God promised believers His deep, abiding joy—*not*
fleeting happiness, which is here today, gone tomorrow. The joy of the
Lord rises above external situations and supernaturally overshadows
everything else to become our inexplicable, internal strength.

Morning
A Love That Remains

"Remain in me, as I also remain in you. No branch
can bear fruit by itself; it must remain in the vine.
Neither can you bear fruit unless you remain in me."
JOHN 15:4 NIV

Want to know how to have a love that remains? One that will never die?
Remain in the Lord. Abide in Him. If you're in a fruitless season of your
life, double-check to make sure you're still connected to the Life-Giver.
Once you're grafted into the vine, fruit will grow—and love will flow!

Evening
Knowing God

Whoever does not love does not
know God, because God is love.
1 JOHN 4:8 NIV

Love isn't always easy, is it? Sometimes it's tough to extend love,
particularly when our feelings are hurt or we're wounded in some way.
The Bible is clear that God is love. He epitomizes it, in fact. And if we
withhold our love from others, even if we feel justified, we break God's
heart. If we claim to know Him, we have no choice but to love.

Morning
Extraordinary Blessing

There shall be showers of blessing.
EZEKIEL 34:26 KJV

Don't you enjoy walking through seasons of extraordinary blessing?
We can hardly believe it when God's "more than enough" provision
shines down upon us. What did we do to deserve it? Nothing!
During such seasons, we can't forget to thank Him for the many
ways He is moving in our lives. Our hearts must overflow with
gratitude to a gracious and almighty God.

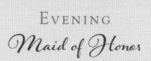

Evening
Maid of Honor

*For I fully expect and hope that…my life will
bring honor to Christ, whether I live or I die.*
PHILIPPIANS 1:20 NLT

Honor. A word not as respected in our society as it once was.
In these days of suggestive attire, cohabitation without marriage,
and tolerance for every behavior imaginable, it's hard to remember
what *honor* means. As Christians, our hope and expectation is to
honor Christ with our lives—especially in the details—because
we are the only reflection of Jesus some people might ever see.

Morning
It's Your Choice

"If you refuse to serve the LORD,
then choose today whom you will serve."
JOSHUA 24:15 NLT

What a wonderful privilege that we get to choose so many things in life! We choose whom we marry, where we live, what church we go to, what outfit we wear. Above all of those things, however, is life's most important choice: choosing to serve the Lord. Today He reaches out with arms of love. Will you respond to that love? It's your choice.

Evening
Giving Your Best

" 'You must present as the LORD's portion the best
and holiest part of everything given to you.' "
NUMBERS 18:29 NIV

Christians are called to give of their time, talents, and treasures. Think about the time God has given you. What time can you give back, and how? And what about your talents? Ask the Lord to show you how to use them to advance the kingdom. And your treasures? If you're struggling with giving to your local church, make this the day you release your hold on your finances. Give the Lord your very best.

MORNING
Focus Point

Therefore. . .stand firm. Let nothing move you.
1 CORINTHIANS 15:58 NIV

Some days stress comes at us from all directions. Our emotions
are overwhelming. Life makes us dizzy. On days like that,
don't worry about getting a lot accomplished—and don't try
to make enormous leaps in your spiritual life. Instead, simply
stand in one place. Like a ballet dancer who looks at one point
to keep her balance while she twirls, fix your eyes on Jesus.

EVENING
He Is Able

The prospect of the righteous is joy.
PROVERBS 10:28 NIV

Living joyfully isn't denying reality. The righteous do not receive
a "Get Out of Pain Free" card when they place their trust in Christ.
We all have hurts in our lives. Some we think we cannot possibly
endure. But even in the midst of our darkest times, our heavenly
Father is able to reach in with gentle fingers to touch us and infuse
us with joy that defies explanation. Impossible? Perhaps by the
world's standards. Yet He is *able*.

Morning
Deep Joy

The Lord is my strength and my shield; my heart trusts in him,
and he helps me. My heart leaps for joy and with my song I praise him.
Psalm 28:7 niv

Sometimes our sorrows run deep. We can feel buried alive. That's why it's so important to allow our joys to run deep, too. Today, as you ponder the many things you have to be thankful for, pause a moment. Take a comforting breath. Thank God from the bottom of your heart for the deep joys in your life.

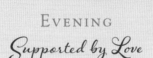

Evening
Supported by Love

When I said, "My foot is slipping," your unfailing love, Lord, supported me.
When anxiety was great within me, your consolation brought me joy.
Psalm 94:18–19 niv

Do you ever feel like slipping when you're around an unlovable person? To say the wrong thing? To let the other person have it? Some people really are harder to love than others, but God's brand of love guards itself against the slippery slope of anger. Next time you feel like snapping, ask the Lord for His perspective. He can refill your love tank in a hurry!

MORNING

Dress for Success

And over all these virtues put on love,
which binds them all together in perfect unity.
COLOSSIANS 3:14 NIV

Have you ever considered that love is part of your wardrobe?
In the same way that you slip on a blouse or a pair of slacks,
you can dress yourself in love each day. And adding love to the
wardrobe means you're truly dressed for success. It's not always easy.
In fact, you have to choose to wear love, much as you would
choose your shoes. It's always the right choice!

EVENING

The Sam Creed

If we are thrown into the blazing furnace, the God whom we serve is able
to save us. . . . But even if he doesn't, we want to make it clear to you,
Your Majesty, that we will never serve your gods.
DANIEL 3:17–18 NLT

Shadrach, Meshach, and Abednego were Israeli boys who had
been raised to worship God before being captured and transported
as slaves to Babylon. Ordered by their new king to worship
his god or die horribly in a fiery furnace, the boys evoked the
SAM Creed, an acronym for their names: my God is able to deliver
me, but even if He chooses not to, I will still follow Him.
Through tough times, let's resolve to live by the SAM Creed.

MORNING
Joy in Unity

*Then make my joy complete by being like-minded,
having the same love, being one in spirit and of one mind.*
PHILIPPIANS 2:2 NIV

Want to know how to bring joy to God's heart? Live in unity with your Christian brothers and sisters. When we're like-minded, it pleases our heavenly Father. Are there problems to be ironed out with a Christian friend? Troubles in your church family? Let this be the day you fulfill His joy by resolving those differences. Let unity lead the way!

EVENING
The Gift of Giving. . .in Secret

*For they gave according to their means, as I can testify,
and beyond their means, of their own accord.*
2 CORINTHIANS 8:3 ESV

Have you ever felt like giving, just to bless someone? Just to bring joy to a friend's heart? Just to lift a burden? There's something rather exciting about giving in secret, isn't there? And when you reach way down deep giving out of your own need it's even more fun. Today, take inventory of the people in your life. Who can you bless. . .in secret?

MORNING
A Moment-to-Moment Choice

Love is a choice you make from moment to moment.
BARBARA DE ANGELIS

Can you hear the ticking of the clock as the seconds pass by? Blink and another second is gone! Turn your head for a moment and you've lost it. In just that amount of time—a blink of an eye—you can choose to love. It is a choice, you know. You can choose to love even the most unlovable person. Don't let another minute tick by. Choose love.

EVENING
Perfect Love

Love never gives up, never loses faith, is always hopeful, and endures through every circumstance.
1 CORINTHIANS 13:7 NLT

We have relationships in three directions: upward (with God), outward (with others), and inward (with ourselves). We are bound to be disappointed at one time or another by the latter two. Because of human frailty, we will inevitably experience failure by others and even ourselves. Our imperfect love will be strained to the breaking point. But our Creator will never fail us—His perfect love truly *never* gives up on us.

MORNING
Infectious Joy

*How lovely on the mountains are the feet of him who brings good news,
who announces peace and brings good news of happiness.*
ISAIAH 52:7 NASB

Ever had a contagious sickness? Something like chicken pox or measles?
Maybe a bad cold? Surely you did your best *not* to share it with your
friends and coworkers. Joy is a lot like that. It's contagious. You can
spread it without even meaning to. Pretty soon all of your Christian
brothers and sisters are catching it. Now, that's one virus you don't
need to worry about. . .so, spread the joy!

EVENING
Because of His Great Love

*But because of his great love for us, God, who is rich in mercy,
made us alive with Christ even when we were dead in
transgressions—it is by grace you have been saved.*
EPHESIANS 2:4–5 NIV

Sometimes we just don't feel like loving. We not only withhold love, but
we punish others by not forgiving them for what they have done to us.
This brings a rift in our relationships, and it isn't good for us. Love acts as
a buffer. God extended mercy to us. Why? Because of His great love. We
must love, even in the hard times, so that mercy and grace can follow.

MORNING
As I Have Loved You

*"A new commandment I give to you, that you love one another,
even as I have loved you, that you also love one another."*
JOHN 13:34 NASB

Why do you suppose Jesus had to command His followers to love one
another? Seems a little sad, doesn't it? You would think that loving
others would come naturally. But Jesus realizes we don't always have it in
us to offer the same kind of love that He offers. His love is life changing.
Oh, that we could extend life-changing love to the world around us!

EVENING
Loose Lips

*We all make many mistakes. For if we could control our tongues,
we would be perfect and could also control ourselves in every other way.*
JAMES 3:2 NLT

Many of us don't let thoughts marinate long before we spew them out
of our mouths. We want to honor God with our speech but seem to
spend more time dousing forest fires resulting from sparks kindled by
our wagging tongues (James 3:5). Don't despair! There's hope for loose
lips! The Creator of self-control is happy to loan us a muzzle
(Psalm 39:1) if we sincerely want to change.

MORNING
Grounded in Love

*"You'll be built solid, grounded in righteousness,
far from any trouble—nothing to fear!"*
ISAIAH 54:12 MSG

Balance isn't something we can achieve in ourselves. Just when we
think we have it all together, life has a tendency to come crashing down
around our ears. But even in the midst of life's most chaotic moments,
God gives us grace; He keeps us balanced in His love. Like a building
that is built to sway in an earthquake without falling down, we will stay
standing if we remain grounded in His love.

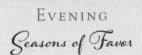

EVENING
Seasons of Favor

*May those who delight in my vindication shout for joy
and gladness; may they always say, "The LORD be exalted,
who delights in the well-being of his servant."*
PSALM 35:27 NIV

Do you ever feel like God's favorite child? Ever marvel at the fact
that He continues to bestow His extraordinary favor upon you,
even when you don't deserve it? God takes great pleasure in you and
wants to bless you above all you could ask or think. So, when you're
in a season of favor, praise Him. Shout for joy and be glad!
Tell others about the great things the Lord has done.

Morning
Joy in Serving

So we, being many, are one body in Christ,
and every one members one of another.
ROMANS 12:5 KJV

There's a lot of work to be done in the local church. Someone has to teach the children, vacuum the floors, prepare meals for the sick, and so forth. With so many needs, how does the body of Christ function without its various members feeling taken advantage of? If you're in a position of service at your local church, praise God for the opportunity to serve others. Step out. . .with joy leading the way.

Evening
Lighthouse Love

For God who said, "Light shall shine out of darkness,"
is the One who has shone in our hearts.
2 CORINTHIANS 4:6 NASB

Have you heard the story of the lighthouse keeper's daughter who kept faithful vigil for her sailor? Every night she watched as the light's beam pierced the blackness and sliced through raging storms, driven by relentless hope that her lover would return to her on the morning's tide. God loves us like that. He's our light in the darkness, guiding, beckoning, and filling our hearts with hope. He never tires. He never stops.

MORNING
Shackles of Love

There's nothing more freeing than the shackles of love.
EMMA RACINE DE FLEUR

God never intended that we should live a life feeling imprisoned by anger, frustration, or pain. Love overcomes all of those things! In a manner of speaking, love binds and shackles us, but we don't feel imprisoned. Instead, we are set free! For God's love supersedes even the toughest of challenges and tears down prison walls. Today make a choice to replace the negative shackles in your life with the shackles of love.

EVENING
Follow Hard after God

Take me away with you—let us hurry!
Let the king bring me into his chambers.
SONG OF SONGS 1:4 NIV

Have you ever heard the expression "follow hard after God"? To follow Him with passion means that you can't live without Him. This kind of passionate love between God and His people has been going on since the beginning of time. He longs for you to run into His arms so that His love can bring healing in your life. Hurry into His chambers today! There He awaits with arms extended.

MORNING

Integrity

People with integrity walk safely, but those
who follow crooked paths will be exposed.

PROVERBS 10:9 NLT

Achieving balance in life is seldom easy. We're likely to go too far
in first one direction and then another. But despite our tendency to
wobble, God's grace leads us always forward. He keeps us from staggering
too far off the path. As we follow Him, choosing a path of integrity
rather than one of selfishness and lies, we will find our way easier, our
footing surer, and our balance steadier.

EVENING

Comforting the Comfortless

He comes alongside us when we go through hard times, and before you
know it, he brings us alongside someone else who is going through hard
times so that we can be there for that person just as God was there for us.

2 CORINTHIANS 1:4 MSG

Heartbroken and hollow after my sixth miscarriage, I struggled to find
meaning in my loss. My heavenly Father's arms comforted me when I
burst into tears at song lyrics or at the sight of a mother cuddling her
infant in Walmart. I finally relinquished my babies to Jesus' loving
embrace, confident that I'd see them again one day. Then I was able to
share His comfort and hope with other women suffering miscarriages.

MORNING
Turn, Turn, Turn

To every thing there is a season,
and a time to every purpose under the heaven.
ECCLESIASTES 3:1 KJV

Oh, those changing seasons! We watch in wonder as the vibrant green leaves slowly morph into dry brown ones, eventually losing their grip on the trees and drifting down to the ground below. Change is never easy, particularly when you have to let go of the past. But oh, the joy of recognizing that God sees into the future. He knows that springtime is coming. Our best days are ahead!

EVENING
Finding Favor

But Noah found favor in the eyes of the LORD.
GENESIS 6:8 NIV

Ever wonder why Noah stood out head and shoulders above others in his generation? Why did God look upon him with favor? Noah walked with God and was righteous. Do you have what it takes to be a "Noah" in this generation? Walk with God daily. Don't let the things of this world zap your strength. Trust Him, live for Him, and watch Him rain down favor in your life!

MORNING
Never Forsaken

For the LORD loves the just and will not forsake his faithful ones.
Wrongdoers will be completely destroyed; the offspring of the wicked will perish.
PSALM 37:28 NIV

God loves all of humankind, but it's clear that He has a special place
in His heart for those who call Him "Father." He adores those who are
faithful to Him and who treat others justly. Unlike some earthly fathers,
God never abandons His kids. Never. He will protect us forever.
What an amazing heart of love our Daddy God has for us!

EVENING
Three Little Words

Three things that last forever—faith, hope, and love.
1 CORINTHIANS 13:13 NLT

Don't you get tired of throwing away panty hose? It's hard to believe
that modern technology can scan quivers inside our livers and detect
nickel-sized puddles on Mars, but we still can't manufacture hose that
won't run. Yep, there are precious few things that endure. Only three,
the Bible says. Three things that will never break down, wear out,
or get lost. These are the *only* things worth keeping.

MORNING
New Insight

Your word is a lamp to guide my
feet and a light for my path.
PSALM 119:105 NLT

We sometimes take the scriptures for granted. These ancient words,
though, continue to shine with light just as they did centuries ago.
In them, God's grace is revealed to us. In them, we gain
new insight into ourselves and our lives.

EVENING
Search and Find

"I love all who love me.
Those who search will surely find me."
PROVERBS 8:17 NLT

Isn't it wonderful to know that our love for God is always reciprocated?
We express love. He returns it—and then some. Not so with humans!
But God has the ability to return our love with interest! We could never
outgive Him, no matter how hard we tried. If you're on a search for
love, turn to the One who knows it best—and expresses it most.

MORNING
Good News, Bad News

*And they left the tomb quickly with fear and
great joy and ran to report it to His disciples.*
MATTHEW 28:8 NASB

Ever had a day where all of the news was good? You picked up the
phone. . .good news. Read an e-mail. . .good news. Then, the very
next day, all of the news was bad! How do we make sense of it all?
Even those closest to Jesus went through ups and downs. One moment
they mourned His death. . .the next, celebrated His resurrection.
Whether the news is good or bad choose joy.

EVENING
Wag More

*I am not complaining about having too little.
I have learned to be satisfied with whatever I have.*
PHILIPPIANS 4:11 CEV

I oozed envy as writer buddies received awards, broke sales records, and
snagged lucrative contracts. What about me? Where were my accolades?
It had always been enough to know I was following God's chosen path
for me, but suddenly all I could do was complain. I wanted more.
Then God sent me a sign. Actually, it was a bumper sticker on a passing
car: WAG MORE, BARK LESS. Message received. . .with a smile.

MORNING
For Generations

I inherited your book on living; it's mine forever—what a gift!
And how happy it makes me!

PSALM 119:111 MSG

Think of it! God's Word is ours. We can hear His voice in scripture—
and apply it to our own lives. Generation upon generation
has followed this amazing book of life, and now it is our turn.
In the Bible, each and every day, we find God's grace revealed.

EVENING
"For God So Loved. . ."

For God so loved the world, that he gave his only begotten Son,
that whosoever believeth in him should not perish, but have everlasting life.

JOHN 3:16 KJV

The ultimate expression of love, one that will never be surpassed, took
place when God sent Jesus, His only Son, to die on the cross for our
sins. "For God so loved. . .that He gave. . ." That's what love does. It
gives and gives and gives. Love is sacrifice and in the person of Jesus
Christ we witness the ultimate sacrifice. Today, as you ponder God's
love for you, rejoice in the fact that He gave Himself willingly for you.

MORNING

With All My Heart, Soul, and Mind

*And he said to him, "You shall love the Lord your God with
all your heart and with all your soul and with all your mind.
This is the great and first commandment."*

MATTHEW 22:37–38 ESV

It's one thing to love God with our heart. It's another to love
Him with our mind. To love Him with our mind means that
He controls our thoughts, which inevitably control our actions.
To love God with your mind means your ultimate desire is for
His thoughts to be your thoughts. Spend some time focusing on
loving God with your thoughts today. The reward will be great!

EVENING

New Life

*God is so good, and by raising Jesus from death,
he has given us new life and a hope that lives on.*

1 PETER 1:3 CEV

The words of a song I wrote while pregnant with my first child exult
in the similarities between new physical life and new spiritual life in
Christ: "New life stirs within me now. Like a soft breeze, transforming
me now. It's a miracle of love, precious blessing from above. My heart
has taken wings. . .lift me up!" New life. By the goodness of God,
we can experience this precious transformation no less
miraculous than a baby growing within us.

MORNING
A Song of Praise to Him

Let the children of Zion be joyful in their King.
PSALM 149:2 KJV

Something about the voices of children lifted in joyous praise does something to the heart, doesn't it? Innocent, trusting, filled with pure happiness their songs ring out for all to hear. Can you imagine how God must feel when we, His children, lift our voices, singing praise to Him? How it must warm His heart! What joy we bring our Daddy God when we praise!

EVENING
Overflowing Love

And may the Lord make your love for one another and for all
people grow and overflow, just as our love for you overflows.
1 THESSALONIANS 3:12 NLT

Overfilling a glass can be messy; overfilling your love tank is anything but! God wants us to have overflowing love—for Him, for our fellow believers, and even for those who annoy us. If you ask, the Lord will increase your love for others. Before long, you'll be spilling all over everyone—those you're closest to and those who drive you a little crazy!

MORNING
Just What We Need

*God can pour on the blessings in astonishing ways so that you're ready for
anything and everything, more than just ready to do what needs to be done.*
2 CORINTHIANS 9:8 MSG

Blessings are God's grace visible to us in tangible form. Sometimes they
are so small we nearly overlook them—the sun on our faces, the smile
of a friend, or food on the table—but other times they amaze us.
Day by day, God's grace makes us ready for whatever comes our way.
He gives us exactly what we need.

EVENING
Bigger than Fear

*Having hope will give you courage.
You will be protected and will rest in safety.*
JOB 11:18 NLT

Tossing, turning, sleepless nights: What woman doesn't know
these intimately? Our thoughts race with the "what ifs" and fear steals
our peace. How precious is God's promise that He will rescue us from
nagging, faceless fear and give us courage to *just say no* to anxious
thoughts that threaten to terrorize us at our most vulnerable moments.
He is our hope and protector. He is bigger than fear. Anxiety flees
in His presence. Rest with Him tonight.

MORNING
Joy in the Battle

*Then they returned, every man of Judah and Jerusalem,
and Jehoshaphat in the forefront of them, to go again to Jerusalem
with joy; for the LORD had made them to rejoice over their enemies.*
2 CHRONICLES 20:27 KJV

Enemy forces were just around the bend. Jehoshaphat, king of Judah,
called his people together. After much prayer, he sent the worshippers
(the Levites) to the front lines, singing joyful praises as they went.
The battle was won! When you face your next battle, praise your way
through it! Strength and joy will rise up within you! Prepare for victory!

EVENING
Joyful in Love

*Keep yourselves in the love of God, looking for
the mercy of our Lord Jesus Christ unto eternal life.*
JUDE 21 KJV

When you love the Lord and recognize His great love for you,
it's easy to be joyful! Think of His marvelous deeds. Relish in His
overwhelming love for His children. Recognize His daily blessings.
Oh, may we never forget that the Lord our God longs for us to see
the depth of His love for us. . .and to love Him fully in return.

Morning
Life and Nourishment

*"I, the LORD, am the one who answers your prayers and watches over you.
I am like a green pine tree; your blessings come from me."*
HOSEA 14:8 NCV

Think of it: God is like a tree growing at the center of your life!
In the shade of this tree, you find shelter. This tree is ever green,
with deep roots that draw up life and nourishment. Each one of
life's daily blessings is the fruit of this tree. It is the source of all
your life, all your joy, and all your being.

Evening
Timeout

The LORD will not abandon His people.
1 SAMUEL 12:22 NASB

Do you remember when, as a little girl, you languished alone in
your room as punishment? Or maybe you sat with your nose plastered
to the corner in time-out. It felt like your parents had abandoned you,
didn't it? As adults, we sometimes *feel* abandoned when that's not the
case at all. We're actually in a place strategically chosen by a loving
Father to teach us, broaden us, and improve us in the end.

MORNING
Because We Love Him

"Because he loves me," says the LORD, *"I will rescue him;*
I will protect him, for he acknowledges my name."
PSALM 91:14 NIV

Have you fallen in love with the God of the universe? He desires a
love relationship with you, you know. He longs for you to come into
His presence and to give your heart to Him. When God sees that
you've fallen head over heels for Him, He rushes in to become
your rescuer and protector. This is love's response—to sweep
in and protect. And it's all because you love Him.

EVENING
Chef d'oeuvre

Be strong and let your heart take courage,
all you who hope in the LORD.
PSALM 31:24 NASB

Identical eggs can be turned into greasy fried egg sandwiches or an
exquisite soufflé. The difference is how much beating they endure.
When life seems to be beating us down, we must remember that we
are a masterpiece in progress. The mixing, slicing, and dicing may feel
brutal at times, but our Lord has offered us His courage and strength
to endure until He is ready to unveil the *chef d'oeuvre*.

Morning
Rejoicing in the Hard Times

Yet I will rejoice in the LORD, I will joy in the God of my salvation.
HABAKKUK 3:18 KJV

Perhaps you've been waiting on pins and needles for something to happen, a promised promotion, an amazing opportunity, something wonderful. Instead, you get bad news. Things aren't going to pan out the way you expected. What do you do now? Instead of giving in to disappointment, continue to rejoice in the Lord and watch the disappointment lift. He will replace your sorrows with great joy.

Evening
The Most Excellent Way

I will show you the most excellent way.
If I speak in the tongues of men or of angels, but do not have love,
I am only a resounding gong or a clanging cymbal.
1 CORINTHIANS 12:31–13:1 NIV

If you've ever navigated a rocky path in the dark without a flashlight, you have some small taste of what it would be like to go through life without love. You could probably make it from point A to point B, but what a rough trip! In the scripture above, God shows us the most excellent way to make the journey. Let love light the way!

MORNING
Blessing Others

"Bless those who curse you.
Pray for those who hurt you."
LUKE 6:28 NLT

Not only does God bless us, but we are called to bless others.
God wants to show the world His grace through us. He can do this
when we show our commitment to make God's love real in the world
around us through our words and actions, as well as through our
prayer life. We offer blessings to others when we greet a scowl with a
smile, when we refuse to respond to angry words, and when we
offer understanding to those who are angry and hurt.

EVENING
Joy in His Presence

Splendor and majesty are before him;
strength and joy are in his dwelling place.
1 CHRONICLES 16:27 NIV

In Old Testament days, only the high priest could enter the holy
of holies to spend intimate time with God. However, when Jesus
died on the cross, the veil in the temple was torn in two! We now
have free access to the Holy of Holies, and Jesus bids us enter. . .often!
He longs to spend time with us in that place. And oh, what joy,
when we enter in! Make that choice today.

MORNING
Faithful in Love

*Love the LORD, all his faithful people! The LORD preserves
those who are true to him, but the proud he pays back in full.*
PSALM 31:23 NIV

Being faithful is a natural consequence of loving someone. Because we
love our spouse, we're faithful, no matter the temptation. And we stick
by our family members, even when we disagree with their actions. We're
true to our friends in thick and thin. God wants us to be faithful to Him,
as well. No straying. No playing the field. We're His bride, linked by
love, faithful until He calls us home to heaven.

EVENING
That Morning

*You have placed your faith and hope in God because
he raised Christ from the dead and gave him great glory.*
1 PETER 1:21 NLT

Have you ever wondered how Mary felt that Easter morning when she
discovered Jesus' tomb empty? Already grieving, imagine the shock of
discovering the body of her Savior—the One who held all her hopes
and dreams—gone! How can that be? Maybe. . . ? Hope glimmers.
But no—impossible. He *did* say something about resurrection, but that
was figurative, wasn't it? Who are. . .*You are?* I must run and tell them.
It's true! He has risen! He's alive! My hope lives, too!

MORNING
Showered with Grace

May God's grace be eternally upon
all who love our Lord Jesus Christ.
EPHESIANS 6:24 NLT

Did you know that your love for Jesus has an amazing return? When you love Him, God showers you with grace, not just now, but for eternity. Grace, mercy, and compassion are yours—all because you love Him. What a great deal! Praise the Lord for His love-induced grace!

EVENING
Faith, Hope, and Love

Love never fails. . . . And now these three remain: faith, hope and love.
But the greatest of these is love.
1 CORINTHIANS 13:8, 13 NIV

When everything else fades away to nothingness, love will remain. Think about that for a moment. When this earth as we know it is long gone, God's love for us will remain. All of our possessions, talents, and abilities will fade, but the way we treated others—the love we showed them—will linger forever in their memories. Love people in such a way that they will remember you long after you're gone.

MORNING

Disappointment. . .Be Gone!

And this hope will not lead to disappointment.
ROMANS 5:5 NLT

Tired of being disappointed time and time again? Ready for things to change? Try hope. Hope never leads to disappointment. When you're hopeful, you are anticipating good things, not bad. And even if the "good things" you're waiting on don't happen right away, you're energized with joy until they do. So, wave good-bye to disappointment. Choose hope. Choose joy.

EVENING

Pick Me Up, Daddy

We. . .rejoice in hope of the glory of God.
ROMANS 5:2 KJV

To rejoice means to live joyfully. . .joy-fully. . .full of joy. Joy is a decision we make. A choice *not* to keep wallowing in the mud of our lives. And there will be mud—at one time or another. When spiritual rain mixes with the dirt of fallen people, mud is the inevitable result. The Creator of sparkling sunbeams, soaring eagles, and spectacular fuchsia sunsets wants to lift us out of the mud. Why don't we raise our arms to Him today?

MORNING
Walk Confidently

*"But blessed are those who trust in the LORD
and have made the LORD their hope and confidence."*
JEREMIAH 17:7 NLT

What gives you confidence? Is it your clothes. . .your money. . .your skills? These are all good things, but they are blessings from God, given to you through His grace. When your hopes (in other words, your expectations for the future) rest only in God, then you can walk confidently, knowing He will never disappoint you.

EVENING
Fullness of Joy

*You make known to me the path of life; in your presence there
is fullness of joy; at your right hand are pleasures forevermore.*
PSALM 16:11 ESV

When we stay on God's path we experience fullness in every area. And if we stick close to Him, which we are called to do, we will experience joy not just now, in this life, but forevermore. Can you imagine. . .a joy that never ends? Draw near to the Lord. In His presence you will find fullness of joy.

MORNING
Eternal Joy!

*And the ransomed of the LORD shall return, and come to
Zion with songs and everlasting joy upon their heads: they shall
obtain joy and gladness, and sorrow and sighing shall flee away.*
ISAIAH 35:10 KJV

Have you ever pondered eternity? Forever and ever and ever. . . ?
Our finite minds can't grasp the concept, and yet one thing
we understand from scripture: We will enter eternity in a state
of everlasting joy and gladness. No more tears! No sorrow!
An eternal joy-fest awaits us! Now that's something to celebrate!

EVENING
Patience of Hope

*We call to mind your work of faith, your labor of love, and your patience
of hope in following our Master, Jesus Christ, before God our Father.*
1 THESSALONIANS 1:3 MSG

Labor. The word alone draws a shudder from the most stalwart
of pregnant women. Just as laboring to bring forth new physical life
requires patience, birthing new spiritual life may require an intensive
labor of love: ceaseless prayer. Countless mothers on their knees
praying for the salvation of a loved one have rejoiced in answered
prayer. Their secret? *Patience of hope.*

MORNING
Look Up!

The heavens declare the glory of God;
the skies proclaim the work of his hands.

PSALM 19:1 NIV

Grace is as near as the sky over your head. Look up and be reminded
of how wonderful God truly is. The same God who created the sun
and the atmosphere, the stars and the galaxies, the same God
who day by day creates a new sunrise and a new sunset, that same
God loves you and creates beauty in your life each day!

EVENING
The Debt of Love

Let no debt remain outstanding, except the continuing debt to love
one another, for he who ever loves others has fulfilled the law.

ROMANS 13:8 NIV

If you've ever taken out a loan for a car or house, you know the
woes of being indebted to someone else. It's not a great feeling, is it?
There is one debt, however, that isn't hard to carry. It's the debt
of love. Anger and strife can destroy relationships, but when the debt
of love is paid, hearts are mended and pain is vanquished.
May your only debt be the debt of love!

Morning
Joyous Heirs

*That being justified by his grace, we should be
made heirs according to the hope of eternal life.*
TITUS 3:7 KJV

Have you ever been the recipient of an inheritance?
Ever had a family member pass away, leaving you money or
objects? There is an inheritance that far exceeds anything we
could ever receive in this world. By God's grace, we are His heirs!
What do we inherit? Eternal life! If you haven't already done so,
place your trust in Christ today and experience the joy of
becoming His child. Oh, the joy of a godly inheritance!

Evening
Dwelling Place

*Do you not know that you are a temple of
God and that the Spirit of God dwells in you?*
1 CORINTHIANS 3:16 NASB

Have you ever been awed by the beauty of a majestic cathedral
with towering ceilings inlaid with gold and silver, magnificent
paintings, rich carpets, and stained glass windows? Only the finest
for the house of God Almighty. Did you know God thinks of you
and me as living cathedrals—dwelling places of His Spirit?
How amazing to be considered worthy of such an honor!
How immeasurable His love to choose us as His dwelling place!

MORNING

Beautiful World

"Walk out into the fields and look at the wildflowers."
MATTHEW 6:28 MSG

Take the time to go outdoors. Look at nature. You don't have to spend hours to realize how beautiful God made the world. A single flower, if you really look at it, could be enough to fill you with awe. Sometimes we only need something very simple to remind us of God's grace.

EVENING

Joyous Refreshing

"Repent, then, and turn to God, so that your sins may be wiped out, that times of refreshing may come from the Lord."
ACTS 3:19 NIV

Think of a chalkboard, like the one your teacher used in school. What if every bad thing you'd ever done was written on the board? (Shivers!) Now envision the teacher taking the eraser and blotting it all out. Wiping it away. As you watch those sins disappear, you are flooded with joy. Your soul is refreshed. The past no longer holds you back. Give your heart to the Lord, and watch the refreshing come!

MORNING

His Banner over Me Is Love

*"He has brought me to his banquet hall,
and his banner over me is love."*
SONG OF SOLOMON 2:4 NASB

Remember the song from childhood: "His banner over me is love!"
The only love that comes close in this lifetime is the love found
between a husband and wife. When the two are joined as one,
you enter a "banquet hall," where two become one in every sense
of the word. There, in that intimate place, you share all of life's
joys and sorrows—together.

EVENING

Bigger and Better

*Waiting does not diminish us, any more than waiting
diminishes a pregnant mother. We are enlarged in the waiting.
We, of course, don't see what is enlarging us. But the longer we wait,
the larger we become, and the more joyful our expectancy.*
ROMANS 8:24–25 MSG

Life is filled with waiting—on slow people, transportation, doctor
reports, even for God to act. Waiting often requires patience we don't
have. It feels like perpetual pregnancy—anticipating a baby that is never
delivered. The secret is to clasp hands with our Lord. He offers His shield
of protection from sinful attitudes like impatience, irritability, and anger
and replaces them with self-control, kindness, and even joy.
Waiting is inevitable, but we can draw closer to the Father in the waiting.

MORNING
The Fruit of the Spirit

But the fruit of the Spirit is love, joy, peace,
longsuffering, gentleness, goodness, faith.
GALATIANS 5:22 KJV

Want to know how to have the ideal family environment?
Want to see parents living in peace with the teens, and vice versa?
To obtain a joyous family environment, you've got to have a
fruit-bowl mentality. Dealing with anger? Reach inside the bowl for
peace. Struggling with impatience? Grab a slice of long-suffering.
Having a problem with depression? Reach for joy.
Keep that fruit bowl close by! It's going to come in handy!

EVENING
Feed My Lambs

When they had finished eating, Jesus said to Simon Peter, "Simon son
of John, do you love me more than these?" "Yes, Lord," he said,
"you know that I love you." Jesus said, "Feed my lambs."
JOHN 21:15 NIV

What an earthshaking question Jesus asked Peter, His beloved disciple.
"Peter, do you love me more than these?" How would you answer that
question? Surely you would cry out, as Peter did, "Yes, Lord! You know
I do!" But Jesus' response to His followers will always be the same:
"If you love me, care for my children." We're forever indebted
to love others in the body of Christ.

MORNING
Law of Love

I pondered the direction of my life,
and I turned to follow your laws.
PSALM 119:59 NLT

Did you know that the word *law* comes from root words that mean "foundation" or "something firm and fixed"? Sometimes we can't help but feel confused and uncertain. When that happens, turn to God's law, His rule for living. Love is His law, the foundation that always holds firm. When we cling to that, we find direction.

EVENING
Going the Distance

[David]. . .chose five smooth stones from the stream. . .
and, with his sling in his hand, approached the Philistine.
1 SAMUEL 17:40 NIV

That little dude David had no intention of backing down from his fight until it was finished. Notice he picked up *five* rocks, not just one. He was prepared to go the distance against his giant. He fully expected God to make him victorious, but he knew it wouldn't be easy. So you've used your first rock against your giant. Maybe even your second. But don't give up. Keep reloading your sling and go the distance. Victory is sweet!

DAY 62

MORNING

As You Love Yourself

Each one of you also must love his wife as he loves himself,
and the wife must respect her husband.

EPHESIANS 5:33 NIV

Husbands are taught by scripture to love their wives as they love themselves. There's nothing more motivating to a wife than the genuine love of a godly husband, one who would be willing to lay down his life for her. It propels her to be the best possible wife she can be. Respect comes easy for a man who loves like that!

EVENING

Joyous Endurance

Behold, we count them happy which endure. Ye have heard
of the patience of Job, and have seen the end of the Lord;
that the Lord is very pitiful, and of tender mercy.

JAMES 5:11 KJV

It's interesting to think of the words *happy* and *endure* in the same sentence. Twenty-first-century Christians are accustomed to a fast-paced life, used to getting what they want when they want it. But sometimes patience is required, especially when we're not feeling well. Want to know the secret of surviving the seasons that try your patience, the ones that wear you to a frazzle? Endure! And happiness will prevail!

Morning
Joy in Forgiveness

Be kind to each other, tenderhearted, forgiving one another,
just as God through Christ has forgiven you.
EPHESIANS 4:32 NLT

Forgiveness is an interesting thing. When you release someone
from the sin he or she has committed against you, it's almost like
setting a bird free from a cage. You've freed that person up to soar.
And, in doing so, you've also freed yourself up. No longer do you
have to hold on to the bitterness or anger. Letting go means you
can truly move forward with your life. . .in joy!

Evening
Wait Just a Minute

We wait in hope for the LORD;
he is our help and our shield.
PSALM 33:20 NIV

Impatience: archenemy of women. Like Batman's Riddler, or Superman's
Lex Luther, impatience stalks us, plots our demise, and blindsides us
via thoughtless neighbors, inconsiderate drivers, careless clerks, dense
husbands, children taking for–ev–er. But waiting is an unavoidable part
of life, and the Bible says we don't have to be undone by it. The Lord's
patience is our shield and defense, and He's got plenty stockpiled.

MORNING
Sound Advice

Without good direction, people lose their way;
the more wise counsel you follow, the better your chances.
PROVERBS 11:14 MSG

Often God makes use of other people when He wants to guide you. His grace flows to you through others' experiences and wisdom. Keep your ears open for His voice speaking to you through the good advice of those you trust.

EVENING
A Loving Proclamation

"Therefore, my friends, I want you to know that through
Jesus the forgiveness of sins is proclaimed to you."
ACTS 13:38 NIV

Through Jesus, God offers forgiveness of sins. Think about that for a minute. He has indebted Himself to humankind through Jesus' work on the cross. He paid the debt for our sin! In doing so, God has made a covenant with us: "Love My Son. Accept His free gift of salvation. In exchange, I will offer you forgiveness of sins and eternal life." Oh, what a gift! What a debt of love He paid!

Morning
"Forgive Us Our Debts"

"'Forgive us our debts, as we also have forgiven our debtors.'"
MATTHEW 6:12 NIV

Is it true that God only forgives us to the extent that we forgive others? That's what the scripture teaches! It's so important not to hold a grudge. It hurts you, and it hurts the one you're refusing to forgive. If you've been holding someone in unforgiveness, may today be the day when you let it go. There is incredible joy both in forgiving and *being* forgiven.

Evening
Jets and Submarines

No power in the sky above or in the earth below—
indeed, nothing in all creation will ever be able to separate us
from the love of God that is revealed in Christ Jesus our Lord.
ROMANS 8:39 NLT

Have you ever been diving amid the spectacular array of vivid color and teeming life in the silent world under the sea? Painted fish of rainbow hues are backlit by diffused sunbeams. Multi-textured coral dot the gleaming white sand. You honestly feel as if you're in another world. But every world is God's world. He soars above the clouds with us and spans the depths of the seas. *Nothing* can separate us from His love.

Morning
Grace for Each Day

*May the Lord direct your hearts into
God's love and Christ's perseverance.*
2 Thessalonians 3:5 niv

Allow God to lead you each day. His grace will lead you deeper
and deeper into the love of God—a love that heals your wounds
and works through you to touch those around you. Just as Christ
never gave up but let love lead Him all the way to the cross, so,
too, God will direct you all the way, giving you the strength
and the courage you need to face each challenge.

Evening
The Prayer of Faith

*And the prayer of faith shall save the sick,
and the Lord shall raise him up.*
James 5:15 kjv

Have you ever wondered why God instructed church leaders to pray
for the sick? Perhaps it's because, when we're sick, we often don't
have the strength to pray for ourselves. We need our brothers and
sisters in the Lord to cry out on our behalf. If you're struggling with
illness, call for your Christian friends or church leaders to come
and pray with you. What joy. . .when healing comes!

MORNING
Incomprehensible Love

There are three things that amaze me—no, four things that I don't understand: how an eagle glides through the sky, how a snake slithers on a rock, how a ship navigates the ocean, how a man loves a woman.
PROVERBS 30:18–19 NLT

The love between a man and woman is a wondrous thing. It's God-breathed. When two people are in love, they can't see straight. Nothing else exists! God designed us to share this amazing, toe-tapping, heart-singing love. It's inexplicable and often defies reason, but that's the beauty of it. Some things just aren't meant to be understood—just experienced.

EVENING
Please Rescue Me

I long for you to rescue me! Your word is my only hope.
PSALM 119:81 CEV

Have you ever longed to be rescued? Stranded after shredding knee ligaments during a remote mountain skiing accident, I waited helplessly for rescuers to arrive. All alone on the raw Canadian mountainside, I felt fear mount. Freezing temperatures, prowling cougars, and unrelenting pain threatened to engulf me in despair. So I did the most and the least I could do: I prayed and recited scripture. And my faithful heavenly Father rescued me with His peace.

MORNING
Joyous Freedom

Blessed is he whose transgression is forgiven,
whose sin is covered.
PSALM 32:1 KJV

What if you were locked up in a prison cell for years on end? You waited for the day when the jailer would turn that key in the lock releasing you once and for all. In a sense, experiencing God's forgiveness is like being set free from prison. Can you fathom the joy? Walking into the sunshine for the first time in years? Oh, praise Him for His forgiveness today!

EVENING
I Have Come That You Might Have Life

A thief comes only to rob, kill, and destroy.
I came so that everyone would have life, and have it in its fullest.
JOHN 10:10 CEV

Don't you just love life? It's filled with unexpected and undeserved joys. Sure, not every day is a piece of cake, but we're alive and well today and have hope for tomorrow. God's love for us is so deep that He came to earth so that we could have life. . .and not just any life. He wants us to have abundant life. That's a "more than I could ask or think" life.

MORNING

Closer to Him

"When the Spirit of truth comes, he will guide you into all truth.
He will not speak on his own but will tell you what he has heard."
JOHN 16:13 NLT

God's Spirit is truth. In Him there are no lies. You can trust Him absolutely to lead you ever closer to God. This is how you recognize true grace: it will always bring you nearer to the One who loves you most, the God who created you and gave Himself for you. If you find yourself somewhere else, you have not been following the Spirit.

EVENING

They're Just Men

He may have a great army, but they are merely men.
We have the LORD our God to help us and to fight our battles for us!
2 CHRONICLES 32:8 NLT

When facing attack from an enemy army, Hezekiah uttered these profound words: "They're *just* men. The God of All Creation is standing by to fight for us! No comparison!" And sure enough, against all human reasoning, God sent an angel to defeat the entire enemy army (2 Chronicles 32:21). God still intervenes today to help us fight our battles, whether supernaturally or by natural means. Trust Him. He's got His armor on.

MORNING
Love in the House

*Better a small serving of vegetables with
love than a fattened calf with hatred.*
PROVERBS 15:17 NIV

We often think that material possessions can buy happiness. Nothing is further from the truth. What good would it serve if you had everything but couldn't get along with the people in your own household? How sad that would be. It would be better to toss the fancy car and expensive house and learn to love your family the way God loves them. It might be challenging, but the end result would make it all worthwhile.

EVENING
Childlike Hope

*For you have been my hope, Sovereign LORD,
my confidence since my youth.*
PSALM 71:5 NIV

Remember how, as a child, you waited on pins and needles for Christmas to come? You hoped against hope you would get those toys you asked for. You knew in your knower that good things were coming. That same level of expectation can motivate you as an adult. Your Father wants you to trust Him with childlike faith. Put your trust in Him. . .and watch how He moves on your behalf.

MORNING
The Capacity to Forgive

Then Peter came to him and asked, "Lord, how often should
I forgive someone who sins against me? Seven times?"
"No, not seven times," Jesus replied, "but seventy times seven!"
MATTHEW 18:21–22 NLT

It's easy to get fed up with people who repeatedly hurt you and
then ask for forgiveness. We grow weary with their promise that
they won't do it again. If someone has repeatedly hurt you, ask the
Lord to give you wisdom regarding the relationship, then ask Him to
give you the capacity to forgive, even when it seems impossible.
Surely joy will rise up in your soul as you watch God at work.

EVENING
Guilt-Free

I will forgive their wickedness,
and I will never again remember their sins.
HEBREWS 8:12 NLT

Guilt. It tends to consume us women to the point that 90
percent of the things we do are motivated by guilt. But God says
we don't have to allow guilt to control us. We should learn from
past mistakes, certainly, and then shed the guilt like a moth-eaten
winter coat. Don a fresh spring outfit and look ahead. Our past
prepares us for the future if we are open to the present.

Morning

Leading

*But since we belong to the day, let us be sober, putting on
faith and love as a breastplate, and the hope of salvation as a helmet.*
1 Thessalonians 5:8 niv

We sometimes think of discipline as a negative thing, as something
that asks us to sacrifice and punish ourselves. But really the word has
more to do with the grace we receive from instruction and learning,
from following a master. Like an athlete who follows her coach's
leading, we are called to follow our Master, wearing His uniform
of love and His helmet of hope.

Evening

Loving Life!

*Does anyone want to live a life that is long and prosperous?
Then keep your tongue from speaking evil and your lips from telling lies!*
Psalm 34:12–13 nlt

How blessed we are to be alive during the twenty-first century!
We have much available to us and many things to enjoy. If you
want to go on enjoying life for years to come, then spend your
time loving others. Guard your tongue and treat people as you
would like to be treated. Be honest in all you do. Your passion
for life will increase as you speak words of love over others.

MORNING
Saved by Love

By faith Noah, when warned about things not yet seen in holy
fear built an ark to save his family. By his faith he condemned
the world and became heir of the righteousness that is in keeping with faith.
HEBREWS 11:7 NIV

There's a great story in the Bible about Noah—a righteous man chosen by God to save humankind by building an ark. Noah and his family climbed aboard the monstrous boat and escaped the floodwaters. Why did God choose Noah? Because he was a righteous man. Humankind was saved by God's love, not just on the ark, but when God sent His Son, Jesus, to rescue us from sin.

EVENING
When I'm Baaad

"I am the good shepherd; I know my own sheep, and they know me,
just as my Father knows me and I know the Father."
JOHN 10:14–15 NLT

Ever spent much time around sheep? They're really self-centered. All they think about is eating, sleeping, and avoiding conflict. A lot like me. But one good thing about sheep is that they'll drop everything and respond to their shepherd's voice. Not anybody else's voice, just the familiar tones of their own shepherd they've learned to trust and follow. This little ewe wants to recognize and respond to her beloved Shepherd's voice, too. How about you, ewe?

MORNING

Joyous Friendships

*The sweet smell of perfume and oils is pleasant,
and so is good advice from a friend.*
PROVERBS 27:9 NCV

Friendship is a wonderful gift from God. A good friend leaves behind a "pleasant scent." And when you find a friend who offers wise counsel, you are doubly blessed! Today, don't just seek to *find* a friend like that; seek to *be* a friend like that. Leave behind a pleasant aroma to those God has placed in your life.

EVENING

I Will Rejoice!

*This is the day the LORD has made.
We will rejoice and be glad in it.*
PSALM 118:24 NLT

Are you having a hard day? Facing mounting problems? Maybe the bill collectors are calling or the kids are sick. You're at the end of your rope. Pause for a moment and remember: *This is the day which the Lord has brought about. I will rejoice.* It's His day and He longs for you to spend time with Him. Rejoice! It's the right choice.

MORNING
Follow Jesus

"Whoever serves me must follow me; and where I am, my servant also will be. My Father will honor the one who serves me."
JOHN 12:26 NIV

A disciple is someone who follows. That is the discipline we practice: we follow Jesus. Wherever He is, we go. In His presence we find the daily grace we need to live. As we serve Him, God honors us; He affirms our dignity and makes us all we were meant to be.

EVENING
Climb In

May the God of hope fill you with all joy and peace as you trust in him, so that you may overflow with hope by the power of the Holy Spirit.
ROMANS 15:13 NIV

Trust is the bottom line when it comes to living an abundant life. We will never escape the muddy ruts without trusting that God has the leverage and power to pull us out of the quagmire. They say faith is like believing the tight rope walker can cross the gorge pushing a wheelbarrow. Trust is climbing into his wheelbarrow. Only when we climb into God's wheelbarrow can His joy and peace overflow as hope into our hearts.

MORNING
Around the Clock Love

A friend loves at all times,
and a brother is born for a time of adversity.
PROVERBS 17:17 NIV

Have you ever considered the idea that a friend loves at all times?
Seems impossible, doesn't it? Even friends squabble. They don't get
along from time to time. They might even part ways. Still, God longs
for the love to remain intact. Today if you're in a rough season with
a friend, ask the Lord to restore your love. Then be ready to be that
person's friend—24/7.

EVENING
Crowned with Love

Praise the LORD, my soul, and forget not all his benefits—
who forgives all your sins and heals all your diseases, who redeems
your life from the pit and crowns you with love and compassion.
PSALM 103:2–4 NIV

We take many things for granted in this life: our health,
God's provision, our daily bread, the love of family members
and friends, and much more. Oh, may we never forget to praise
our loving God, who showers us with benefits. He forgives our sins.
He redeems us from the pit. And He places a glittering crown
of love and compassion on us, calling us His daughters and sons.

MORNING
Dividing Joy

Tell this news with shouts of joy to the people;
spread it everywhere on earth.
ISAIAH 48:20 NCV

Joy is meant to be shared. (It's hard to keep to yourself, after all!) Think of it like a tasty apple pie. You can't eat the whole thing, can you? No, you need to spread the love, share the slices. So it is with joy. When you're going through a particularly joyful season, pass the plates. Sharing is half the fun!

EVENING
Questions and Answers

And the Scriptures were written to teach
and encourage us by giving us hope.
ROMANS 15:4 CEV

God's Word is brimming with answers to life's difficulties, yet it's often the last place we turn. God speaks to us today through the lives of trusting Abraham, broken-hearted Ruth, runaway Jonah, courageous Esther, female leader Deborah in a male-dominated society, beaten-down Job, double-crossing Peter, and Paul, who proved people *can* change.

Morning
Christlike

Don't sin by letting anger control you.
Think about it overnight and remain silent.
PSALM 4:4 NLT

A disciple must practice certain skills until she becomes good at them.
As Christ's disciples, we are called to live like Him. The challenge of
that calling is often hardest in life's small, daily frustrations, especially
with the people we love the most. But as we practice saying no to anger,
controlling it rather than allowing it to control us, God's grace helps
us develop new skills, even ones we never thought possible!

Evening
A Chorus of Praise

Sing for joy to God our strength;
shout aloud to the God of Jacob!
PSALM 81:1 NIV

Imagine you're in a room filled with noisy, fussy, crying children.
The combination of their voices raised in miserable chorus is
overwhelming. Now imagine that same group of children,
singing praise to God in unison. They're making a joyful noise
and what a pleasant sound it is! Today, as you face life's many
challenges, focus on being a praise-giver, not a fussy child.

MORNING
Brotherly Affection

Let love be genuine. Abhor what is evil; hold fast to what is good. Love one another with brotherly affection. Outdo one another in showing honor.
ROMANS 12:9–10 ESV

Brotherly affection is that "slap on the back," "laugh at the same jokes" kind of love. Affection means caring. When you love, you genuinely care about other people—how they feel, their hopes and dreams, their heartbreaks. Everything about them matters to you because it matters to them. Hold fast to what is good. Love one another!

EVENING
Hope Resurrected

We had hoped that he would be the one to set Israel free! But it has already been three days since all this happened.
LUKE 24:21 CEV

The scenario for this scripture is quite unusual. Two of Jesus' disciples are describing their lost hope due to the events surrounding Jesus' death to none other than Jesus Himself. They don't recognize Him as they walk together on the road to Emmaus after His resurrection. Spiritual cataracts blind them to the hope they thought was dead—right in front of them! Let's open our spiritual eyes to Jesus, who is walking beside us.

MORNING
Greeting One Another in Joy

Speaking to one another with psalms, hymns and songs from the Spirit.
Sing and make music from your heart to the Lord.
EPHESIANS 5:19 NIV

Want to try a fun experiment? The next time someone asks you how you're doing, instead of responding, "Okay," why not get more specific? Try "I'm blessed!" or "Having an awesome day!" Encourage yourself in the Lord and He will keep those spirits lifted. And encourage one another with words of blessing, as well.

EVENING
His Abounding Love

And he passed in front of Moses, proclaiming,
"The LORD, the LORD, the compassionate and gracious God,
slow to anger, abounding in love and faithfulness."
EXODUS 34:6 NIV

Have you ever wondered what it means to be abounding in something? Try replacing the word *abounding* with the word *wealthy*. God is wealthy in love and faithfulness. He has more than enough to share with His kids. Talk about an inheritance! And He wants us to share the love. When we accept Jesus and walk in relationship with Him, we're wealthy with His love. Make a point to share the wealth today.

MORNING
Life's Circumstances

My child, do not reject the LORD's discipline, and don't get angry when he corrects you. The LORD corrects those he loves, just as parents correct the child they delight in.

PROVERBS 3:11–12 NCV

God doesn't send us to time-out, and He certainly doesn't take us over His knee and spank us. Instead, His discipline comes to us through the circumstances of life. By saying yes to whatever we face, no matter how difficult and frustrating it may be, we allow God's grace to infuse each moment of our day. We may be surprised to find that even in life's most discouraging moments, God's love was waiting all along.

EVENING
Girlfriends

And our hope for you is firm, because we know that just as you share in our sufferings, so also you share in our comfort.

2 CORINTHIANS 1:7 NIV

Anne of Green Gables was right: bosom friends are important. Girls need girlfriends. . .little girls and gown-up girls alike. God wired us to need each other, to yearn for the heart-bonding that results from sharing sufferings, comfort, hugs, and giggles. Nothing's wrong with men, of course, but they don't make the same bosom friends as girls. Have you thanked the Lord lately for your soul-sisters?

MORNING
Love Your Brother

Whoever claims to love God yet hates a brother or sister is a liar.
For whoever does not love their brother or sister, whom they have seen,
cannot love God, whom they have not seen. And he has given us this
command: Anyone who loves God must also love their brother and sister.
1 JOHN 4:20–21 NIV

It's interesting to think that we're commanded to love God even though we have never seen Him with our eyes. Stranger still is that we have a hard time loving our brother—friend, neighbor, fellow church member—whom we *have* seen. God's ideal arrangement includes loving both the one we can see and the One we can't.

EVENING
His Mercy Endures Forever

O give thanks unto the LORD; for he is good:
for his mercy endureth for ever.
PSALM 136:1 KJV

God's mercy endures forever. It never ends. What about *our* mercy? How long does it endure? Until our patience is tested? Until someone rubs us the wrong way? Until we're hurt or offended by a friend or coworker? If God's mercy endures forever, we should strive to be merciful, too. After all, if the King of kings offers it repetitively, shouldn't we do so, as well? Today, extend mercy. . .and watch the joy flow!

Morning
A Receipt of Joy

"When I smiled at them, they could hardly believe it;
their faces lit up, their troubles took wing!"
JOB 29:24 MSG

Some folks are natural joy-givers! They thrive on bringing joy to others in their world. If that's your nature, then you need to know that God wants you to *receive* joy, too. It's a dual process. When you give it, like a boomerang, it comes back to you! So, toss out some joy today. It will surely return, filling your heart and bringing a smile to your face!

Evening
Sprouts

"For there is hope for a tree, when it is cut down,
that it will sprout again."
JOB 14:7 NASB

Have you ever battled a stubborn tree? You know, one you can saw off at the ground but the tenacious thing keeps sprouting new growth from the roots? You have to admire the resiliency of that life force, struggling in its refusal to give up. That's hope in a nutshell, sisters. We must believe, even as stumps, that we will eventually become majestic, towering evergreens if we just keep sending out those sprouts.

MORNING
Reach Out to Him

"Your words have supported those who were falling;
you encouraged those with shaky knees."
JOB 4:4 NLT

God knows how weak and shaky we feel some days. He understands our feelings. After all, He made us, so He understands how prone humans are to discouragement. He doesn't blame us for being human, but He never leaves us helpless, either. His grace is always there, like a hand held out to us, simply waiting for us to reach out and grasp it.

EVENING
On the Rebound

But you, Lord, are a compassionate and gracious God,
slow to anger, abounding in love and faithfulness.
PSALM 86:15 NIV

It's interesting to see that God's love is both abounding—and rebounding. It keeps coming around to meet us again, even after we've failed. This is because of His compassionate nature. In the same way, we are expected to rebound (bounce back), even after our love for people is challenged. Don't stay away too long. Come back home to love.

MORNING
Love Your Enemies

"But I say, love your enemies! Pray for those who persecute you!"
MATTHEW 5:44 NLT

We're not just called to love people who love us; we're commanded to love the ones who hurt us—the very ones who bring us grief. How is that possible? First, we have to acknowledge that all of us sin and fall short of the glory of God. Next, we have to let go of any bitterness and pain. Finally, we must pray for our enemies. Only in prayer can love win out.

EVENING
One for All

All of you are part of the same body. There is only one Spirit of God, just as you were given one hope when you were chosen to be God's people.
EPHESIANS 4:4 CEV

Remember the motto of the Three Musketeers? "All for one and one for all." Christ-followers should have the same sense of unity, for we are bound together by eternal hope, the gift of our Savior. Feeling *with* and *for* each other, we'll cry tears of joy from one eye and tears of sadness from the other. Loneliness is not an option. Take the first step. Reach out today—someone else's hand is reaching, too.

MORNING

Pressed Down, Running Over

Give, and it shall be given unto you; good measure, pressed down,
and shaken together, and running over, shall men give into your bosom.
LUKE 6:38 KJV

"Give, and it shall be given unto you." Likely, if you've been walking
with the Lord for any length of time, you've heard this dozens of times.
Do we give so that we can get? No, we give out of a grateful heart, and
the Lord in His generosity meets our needs. Today, pause and thank Him
for the many gifts He has given you. Do you feel the joy running over?

EVENING

Merciful Joy

It is a sin to hate your neighbor,
but being kind to the needy brings happiness.
PROVERBS 14:21 NCV

Our loving heavenly Father is so merciful toward us, and He expects us
to treat others with mercy, too. Did you realize that having mercy on
those who are less fortunate than you can actually make you happy?
It's true! Reach out to someone today and watch the joy start to flow!

MORNING
Reach Out to Others

*Whoever has the gift of encouraging
others should encourage.*
ROMANS 12:8 NCV

Just as God encourages us, He wants us to encourage others. The word *encourage* comes from Latin words that mean "to put heart or inner strength into someone." When God encourages us, His own heart reaches out to us and His strength becomes ours. As we rely on His grace, we are empowered to turn and reach out to those around us, lending them our hearts and strength.

EVENING
Counting On It

*Blessed is the one who perseveres under trial,
because having stood the test, that person will receive the
crown of life that the Lord has promised to those who love him.*
JAMES 1:12 NIV

Some think that when you turn your life over to Christ, troubles are over. But if you've been a believer for more than a day, you'll realize that the Christian life is no Caribbean cruise. There will be trials; there will be tribulations. Count on it. But Jesus promises a glorious reward for our perseverance through those hard times. Count on *that* even more.

DAY 88

The Love Test

If your enemy is hungry, give him bread to eat, and if he is thirsty,
give him water to drink, for you will heap burning coals on his head,
and the LORD will reward you.
PROVERBS 25:21–22 ESV

What would you do if your mortal enemy was in trouble? Say, his house burned down or his child was critically ill? Would you pass the love test? Could you lay your angst aside and extend a hand in his direction, genuinely offering love? Spend some time today asking the Lord to share His plan for sharing love with those who have become enemies. Before long, the walls will come tumbling down!

EVENING
On the Rebound

But you, Lord, are a compassionate and gracious God,
slow to anger, abounding in love and faithfulness.
PSALM 86:15 NIV

It's interesting to see that God's love is both abounding—and rebounding. It keeps coming around to meet us again, even after we've failed. This is because of His compassionate nature. In the same way, we are expected to rebound (bounce back), even after our love for people is challenged. Don't stay away too long.
Come back home to love.

MORNING
Giving Thanks

Let us continually offer the sacrifice of praise to God,
that is, the fruit of our lips, giving thanks to His name.
HEBREWS 13:15 NKJV

What do you think of when you hear the word *giving*? Money? Gifts? Offerings? Time? Talents? Treasures? One of the things we're called to give. . .is thanks! That's right. So, pause a moment and thank God for His many blessings in your life. Feels good to give, doesn't it?

EVENING
Heading Home

We are only foreigners living here on earth for a while.
1 CHRONICLES 29:15 CEV

I quivered on the icy Alps peak, more from fear than cold. Which ski slope was my level (beginner) and which were treacherously advanced? A mistake could be deadly. Panic gripped me; I couldn't read the German signs and no one spoke English. As Christians, we're foreigners on this earth. We don't speak the same language or share the same perspective as nonbelievers. We're only passing through this world on our way to the next. . .heading home.

MORNING

Reciprocal

When we get together, I want to encourage you in your faith,
but I also want to be encouraged by yours.
ROMANS 1:12 NLT

Encouragement is always reciprocal. When we encourage others, we are ourselves encouraged. In the world's economy, we pay a price in order to receive something we want; in other words, we give up something to get something. But in God's economy, we always get back what we give up. We are connected to each other, like parts of a body. Whatever good things we do for another are good for us, as well.

EVENING

Fresh Mercy

The faithful love of the LORD never ends! His mercies never cease.
Great is his faithfulness; his mercies begin afresh each morning.
LAMENTATIONS 3:22–23 NLT

Don't you love the newness of morning? The dew on the grass? The awakening of the sun? The quiet stillness of the day, when you can spend time alone with the Lord in solitude? Oh, what joy rises in our souls as we realize that God's love and mercy are new every morning! Each day is a fresh start, a new chance. Grace washes over us afresh, like the morning dew. Great is His faithfulness!

MORNING
A Directed Heart

May the Lord direct your hearts into the
love of God and into the steadfastness of Christ.
2 THESSALONIANS 3:5 NASB

God longs for us to be directed, not by emotion, but by His love
and the steadfastness of His Son. When we allow our hearts to
be directed by God's amazing love, we really can deal with our
enemies in a godly way. We have to slow down, take a deep breath,
and listen for God's voice. Only then can we sense His direction
and respond with His love leading the way.

EVENING
Sprung

Because of the covenant I made with you, sealed with blood,
I will free your prisoners from death in a waterless dungeon.
Come back to the place of safety, all you prisoners who still have hope!
ZECHARIAH 9:11–12 NLT

Have you ever felt trapped in a prison of hopelessness? Financial
difficulties, poor health, unemployment, rocky marriage, delinquent
children—there are countless dungeons that shackle us. But God
promises hope and freedom from our prisons. Jesus bailed us out!

MORNING
Joy Comes in the Morning

For his anger lasts only a moment, but his favor lasts a lifetime!
Weeping may last through the night, but joy comes with the morning.
PSALM 30:5 NLT

Can you picture a lifetime of blessing? Hard to imagine, isn't it?
We think of "seasons" of blessing, but God continually pours out His
favor upon His children. We have our ups and downs our sorrows and
our joys but God remains consistent, never changing. We weep in the
bad times and celebrate during the good. Oh, if only we could remember
that on the tail end of every sorrow, there is a joyful tomorrow!

EVENING
A Savior Who Understands

While he was still speaking, there came a crowd, and the man called Judas,
one of the twelve, was leading them. He drew near to Jesus to kiss him.
LUKE 22:47 ESV

Have you ever been betrayed by someone you thought you could trust?
Jesus can relate. Imagine how He must have felt watching one of the
disciples He loved turn on Him and sell Him out for thirty pieces of silver.
Perhaps you feel as if you've been sold out by a friend or loved one. Follow
the example of Jesus, who, even in the face of betrayal, chose to forgive.

Morning
God's Word

I weep with sorrow; encourage me by your word.
Psalm 119:28 NLT

Tears come easily some days. The world is full of pain and darkness, and we feel helpless. Those are the days when we need to turn to God's Word for encouragement. We may not be able to sense His grace in our lives, but we will always find it in the Bible's pages.

Evening
Never Alone

I am convinced that nothing can ever separate us from God's love. Neither death nor life, neither angels nor demons, neither our fears for today nor our worries about tomorrow—not even the powers of hell can separate us from God's love.
Romans 8:38 NLT

I read a poll that said being alone is one of women's worst fears. When we experience loss, we sometimes feel that we're struggling all alone; that others around us can't possibly comprehend the scope of our fears, our worries, our pain. But the Bible says we're not alone, that *nothing* can separate us from our heavenly Father. He is right there beside us, loving us, offering His companionship when we have none.

MORNING
Love. . .and Do Good

"But I say to you who hear me:
Love your enemies, do good to those who hate you."
LUKE 6:27 ESV

Love is always followed by actions. And not just any actions, either.
When we genuinely love someone, we will respond to him with
kindness. We'll treat him right, even if he doesn't respond similarly.
Love always goes hand in hand with "doing good." Sure, it's hard at
times, but God will give you the strength to get through, so dive in!
Loving others with your actions is the way to go!

EVENING
Joy for the Nations

Therefore the redeemed of the LORD shall return, and come with singing
unto Zion; and everlasting joy shall be upon their head: they shall
obtain gladness and joy; and sorrow and mourning shall flee away.
ISAIAH 51:11 KJV

God longs for people across the globe to turn their hearts to Him.
He wants them to understand that He sent His only begotten Son
to earth to die on a rugged cross so that people of every race, creed,
and color could be set free from their sins. Oh, that people around
the world would turn to God, would return to Him with singing,
and with everlasting joy upon their heads!

MORNING

Joyous Favor

May the favor of the Lord our God rest upon us; establish the work of our hands for us—yes, establish the work of our hands.
PSALM 90:17 NIV

It's interesting to think of "favor" and "the work of our hands" in the same sentence, isn't it? In God's economy, favor equals usefulness. We want the work of our hands to make a difference in this world, and we want to see God smiling down on our ventures. Today, ask God to establish the work of your hands. Then watch as His favor rests upon you!

EVENING

Overflowing Love

Precious in the sight of the LORD is the death of His godly ones.
PSALM 116:15 NASB

Jesus wept. Two small words that portray the enormity of Jesus' emotion following the death of His dear friend, Lazarus (John 11:35). Jesus knew Lazarus wouldn't stay dead, that he'd soon miraculously rise from the grave. So why did Jesus weep? The depth of His love for those precious to Him overflowed. Our Lord grieves with us in our losses today and comforts us with the knowledge that His beloved will rise to eternal life in heaven.

MORNING

By His Grace

A person is made right with God through faith,
not through obeying the law.

ROMANS 3:28 NCV

Human laws can never make us into the people we are meant to be. No matter how scrupulous we try to be, we will always fall short. Our hands and hearts will come up empty. But as we fix our eyes on God, committing our lives and ourselves to Him, we are made right. We are healed and made whole by His grace, exactly as God meant us to be.

EVENING

The Ultimate Betrayal

For while we were still weak,
at the right time Christ died for the ungodly.

ROMANS 5:6 ESV

In spite of humankind's betrayal in the Garden of Eden, the Lord still chose to love us by sending His Son as a sacrifice for our sins. Even now, those of us who follow Jesus slip up and betray Him—with our actions, our thoughts, and our motives. How it must break God's heart! But still He offers love, in spite of His pain. What an amazing example for us to follow.

MORNING
Love's Meditation

Within your temple, O God,
we meditate on your unfailing love.
PSALM 48:9 NIV

Don't you just love corporate worship? There's something about lifting your voice, your hands, and your heart to the King of kings and Lord of lords in the midst of fellow believers. And what an awesome time to meditate on God's unfailing love. As one body, one unit, we come together and recognize the very love that binds us. How wonderful to dwell together—in love!

EVENING
A New Tomorrow

Rahab the harlot...Joshua spared...for she hid the
messengers whom Joshua sent to spy out Jericho.
JOSHUA 6:25 NASB

Rahab was the unlikeliest of heroes: a prostitute who sold her body in the darkest shadows. Yet she was the very person God chose to fulfill His prophecy. How astoundingly freeing! Especially for those of us ashamed of our past or who feel we've strayed too far from God to ever be used by Him. God loved Rahab for who she was—not what she did. Rahab is proof that God can and will use anyone for His higher purposes. *Anyone.* Even you and me.

MORNING
Who Exalts?

No one from the east or the west or from the desert can exalt themselves.
It is God who judges: He brings one down, he exalts another.
PSALM 75:6–7 NIV

Sometimes we grumble when others are exalted. We feel left out.
Why do others prosper when everything around us seems to be falling
apart? We can't celebrate their victories. We aren't joyful for them.
Shame on us! God chooses who to exalt. . .and when. We can't pretend
to know His thoughts. But we can submit to His will and celebrate
with those who are walking through seasons of great favor.

EVENING
Nature's Joyous Song

Let the floods clap their hands:
let the hills be joyful together.
PSALM 98:8 KJV

All of nature sings the praises of our mighty God. Look around you!
Do you see the hills off in the distance, pointing up in majesty?
Can you hear the water in the brooks, tumbling along in a chorus
of praise? And what about the ocean waves? Oh, the joy in discovering
the God of the universe through His marvelous creation!

MORNING
Heartfelt

For we live by believing and not by seeing.
2 CORINTHIANS 5:7 NLT

The world of science tells us that only what can be seen and measured is truly real. But our hearts know differently. Every day, we depend on the things we believe—our faith in God and in our friends and family, our commitment to give ourselves to God and others—and it is these invisible beliefs that give us grace to live.

EVENING
Power Source

*He gives strength to the weary
and increases the power of the weak.*
ISAIAH 40:29 NIV

Sometimes we feel as if our backs will break under the burdens we carry: debt, responsibilities, impossible schedules. But our God promises to strengthen and empower us if we turn to Him for help. He knows. He cares. He is able. It's been written that persecuted European Christians don't pray for God to lessen their loads like American Christians do. They pray for stronger backs instead.

MORNING
Loving His People

God is always fair. He will remember how you helped his people
in the past and how you are still helping them. You belong to God,
and he won't forget the love you have shown his people.
HEBREWS 6:10 CEV

God is watching to see how we treat fellow believers. He's looking down
from His throne in heaven, making sure we're bound together by His
love. When we love, we extend a hand of kindness and friendship. No,
it's not always easy, but it's God's way. And isn't it interesting to read
that God won't forget how we've helped His people? His long-term
memory is wonderful!

EVENING
The Palm of His Hand

If I ride the wings of the morning, if I dwell by the farthest oceans,
even there your hand will guide me, and your strength will support me.
PSALM 139:9–10 NLT

Surf foamed around my ankles as I lifted the burgundy starfish, its pointed
tips curled in taut contraction. "It's okay little fellow, I'll help you,"
I crooned, gently cradling the sea creature stranded by the outgoing tide.
Tiny tentacles tickled my palm as the starfish relaxed, safe and protected.
Likewise, God's hand rescues, supports, and guides us to life-sustaining
waters when we're stranded. We're safe in the palm of His hand.

MORNING
Amazing Love

He remembered his Covenant with them,
and, immense with love, took them by the hand.
PSALM 106:45 MSG

You are loved. . .incredibly, sacrificially loved by the King of kings.
Doesn't that fill you with overwhelming joy? Can you sense His
heart for you? God's love is not based on anything you have done
or will ever do. No, that amazing love was poured out on Calvary
and beckons us daily. You are loved today and always!

EVENING
Covering Offenses

Hatred stirs up strife, but love covers all offenses.
PROVERBS 10:12 ESV

Once you've been betrayed, it's hard to trust again, isn't it? Sure.
Trust needs to be reestablished, rebuilt over time. And our wounds
need time to heal. But even when it's hard to trust, we have to
keep on loving the person who betrayed us. Why? Because love and
trust are two separate things. Trust has to be earned. Love does not.
It covers offenses and tears down walls.

MORNING
Unfailing Love

But I trust in your unfailing love.
I will rejoice because you have rescued me.
PSALM 13:5 NLT

Have you ever done that exercise in trust where you fall backward into another person's arms? It's hard to let yourself drop, trusting that the other person will catch you. The decision to let yourself fall is not an emotion that sweeps over you. It's just something you have to do, despite your fear. In the same way, we commit ourselves to God's unfailing love, finding new joy each time His arms keep us from falling.

EVENING
A Joy Forever

The Mighty One, God, the LORD, speaks and summons
the earth from the rising of the sun to the place where it sets.
From Zion, perfect in beauty, God shines forth.
PSALM 50:1–2 NIV

A child's face. A flowering pear tree. A rippling brook. A mountain's peak. All of these things overwhelm us with the magnitude of their beauty. Why? Because we can see that they were created by Someone much larger than ourselves. Someone incredibly creative and colorful. We are reminded of the awesomeness of God. Focus on the beauty He has placed in your world. . .and praise Him!

MORNING

Built Up by Love

Knowledge puffs up, while love builds up.
1 CORINTHIANS 8:1 NIV

If you're active in the workforce, then you know how tough
it can be to love your fellow workers. More often than not,
we're out to prove that we're better than the next person,
not to shower that person with love. However, sharing God's
love with others at our workplace is really God's plan for us.
Make a decision today to build up your coworkers by loving them.

EVENING

Juiced

God is our refuge and strength,
a very present help in trouble.
PSALM 46:1 NASB

Remember the scene from the movie *Air Force One*,
when Harrison Ford, as the US President, calls for help from
the belly of a terrorist-hijacked plane after much death-defying effort?
Just as the crucial call is dialed, his cell phone battery conks out.
Can you identify? What a relief that our direct line to God—
prayer—is always juiced and never needs recharging!

MORNING
God Rejoices over Me

"The LORD your God is with you, the Mighty Warrior who saves.
He will take great delight in you, in his love he will no longer rebuke you,
but will rejoice over you with singing."
ZEPHANIAH 3:17 NIV

It's fun to picture God celebrating over us, isn't it? Can you imagine? He sings over us! He dances over us. He rejoices over us! What joy floods our souls as we realize our Father God, like a loving daddy, celebrates His love for His children. Today, reflect on the thought that God with great joy in His voice is singing over you.

EVENING
All Have Sinned

For all have sinned and fall short of the glory of God.
ROMANS 3:23 NIV

One of the reasons it's so important for us to continue loving those who have hurt us is because we never know when it might be our turn to be forgiven. Sure, we set out to do the right thing, but even those with the best of intentions slip up and hurt others. Extend love and forgiveness at every turn. You never know when it might be your turn to receive!

MORNING
Safe in Christ

*This is what God commands: that we believe in his Son,
Jesus Christ, and that we love each other, just as he commanded.*
1 JOHN 3:23 NCV

Again and again, the Bible links faith and love. Our human
tendency is to put up walls of selfishness around ourselves,
to protect ourselves at all costs. God asks us instead to believe
daily that we are safe in Christ and to allow ourselves to be
vulnerable as we reach out in love to those around us.

EVENING
Astounding Rescue

*Then I remember something that fills me with hope. The LORD's kindness
never fails! If he had not been merciful, we would have been destroyed.*
LAMENTATIONS 3:21–22 CEV

With our hectic lifestyles, pausing to remember the past isn't
something we do very often. But perhaps we should. Then, when
doubts assault our faith, fears threaten to devour us, and disaster hovers
like a dark cloud, we'll remember God's past loving-kindnesses. Hope
will triumph over despair. Keeping a prayer journal is a wonderful way
to chronicle answered prayer. We'll always remember the times when
God's merciful hands rescued us in astounding ways.

MORNING
Good News for the Nations!

This same Good News that came to you is going out all over the world.
It is bearing fruit everywhere by changing lives, just as it changed
your lives from the day you first heard and understood the
truth about God's wonderful grace.
COLOSSIANS 1:6 NLT

The word *gospel* means good news. We have good news for the nations!
Jesus Christ came and gave His life for all! If you had great news that
affected your children or friends, wouldn't you share it? Of course you
would. The same holds true with the nations. When we develop a love
for the nations (and this is God's heart for us all as believers),
we can't help but share the good news.

EVENING
Out of the Pit

I waited patiently for the LORD. He turned to me and heard my cry.
He lifted me out of the pit of destruction, out of the sticky mud.
He stood me on a rock and made my feet steady.
PSALM 40:1–2 NCV

When you've been living in the pit, you can hardly imagine being
lifted out of it. Oh, the joy of knowing God can bring us out of even
the deepest, darkest pit and place our feet on solid ground. Nothing is
impossible with our Lord! If you're in a dark place today, call out to Him
. . .and watch as He delivers you. He will establish your steps. Praise Him!

MORNING
Love's Consolation

For we have great joy and consolation in thy love.
PHILEMON 7 KJV

Have you ever found yourself in need of consolation? Ever longed for someone to wrap his or her arms of love around you and make everything all right? God *is* that Someone. We can take great consolation in His love, which is unchanging, everlasting, and abounding. Doesn't it bring joy to your heart to see how wide, how deep, and how long the Father's love is for His children?

EVENING
Close to You

I stay close to you, and your powerful arm supports me.
PSALM 63:8 CEV

There's an old saying: "I used to be close to God, but someone moved." If God is the same yesterday, today, and tomorrow, He's not the one going anywhere. So how do we stay close to God? So close that His powerful arm supports, protects, and lifts us up when we're down? Prayer: as a lifestyle, as much a part of ourselves as breathing. Prayer isn't just spiritual punctuation; it's every word of our life story.

MORNING
Sticking Together

Families stick together in all kinds of trouble.
PROVERBS 17:17 MSG

Families can drive you crazy. Whether it's the people with whom you share a house, or the extended family that gets together at holidays and birthdays, family members can be exasperating, even infuriating. When it comes right down to it, though, your family members are the ones who show you God's grace even when life is hard, the ones who stick by you no matter what (even when they make you crazy!).

EVENING
Love Deeply

Above all, love each other deeply,
because love covers over a multitude of sins.
1 PETER 4:8 NIV

It's human nature to withhold forgiveness in order to teach the other person a lesson, but that's not God's way. He doesn't want us to wait too long to forgive. His desire is that we're honest with each other when we're upset. After all, we all sin and fall short. We have to be willing to go the distance and do what it takes to mend fences. How do we accomplish this? Love deeply.

MORNING
Hope for the Nations

In his name the nations will put their hope.
MATTHEW 12:21 NIV

Hope. What a wonderful, precious commodity. When we have hope, we can face today—and tomorrow. And when we have a love for God's people across the planet, even in places where we've never been, we long to offer them hope, as well. But who will share the Good News? We're all called to participate! Through our giving, our "going," and our great love, the Gospel will be spread.

EVENING
One Hunky Verse

To Him who is able to do far more abundantly beyond all that we ask or think, according to the power that works within us, to Him be the glory…forever and ever. Amen.
EPHESIANS 3:20–21 NASB

Don't you just love the *bigness* of this verse? It radiates with the enormity of God—that *nothing* is beyond His scope or power. Read it aloud and savor the words *far more abundantly*. Now repeat "beyond *all* that we ask or think" three times, pondering each word individually. Wow! If there was ever a hunky verse to cast an attitude of gratitude over our day, this is it. Yay God!

Morning
Make a Joyful Noise

Let us come before His presence with thanksgiving,
let us shout joyfully to Him with psalms.

PSALM 95:2 NASB

Sometimes we forget that the Lord loves us to praise joyfully. We get caught up in tradition or maybe we just feel uncomfortable worshipping with abandon. The Lord loves a happy heart, and He truly enjoys it when we make a joyful noise, lifting up our praises (our psalms) for all to hear. So, break out of the box today! Be set free. . .to worship!

Evening
I've Got the Joy!

I will greatly rejoice in the LORD,
my soul shall be joyful in my God.

ISAIAH 61:10 KJV

As children we used to sing, "I've got the joy, joy, joy, joy down in my heart!" We bounced up and down in our seats with great glee. Do you still have that joy? Has it lingered into your adulthood? Do you sense it to the point where you could come bounding from your chair, ready to share what He's given you with a lost and dying world? Oh, for such a childlike joy!

MORNING
Family Ties

Jesus, who makes people holy, and those who are made holy are from the same family. So he is not ashamed to call them his brothers and sisters.
HEBREWS 2:11 NCV

You and Jesus are family! Jesus, the One who made you whole and clean in God's sight, is your Brother. Family ties connect you to Him and to all those with whom He is connected. In Christ, we find new connections with each other. By His grace, we are now kinfolk.

EVENING
Slip-Sliding Away

Instruct those who are rich in this present world not to be conceited or to fix their hope on the uncertainty of riches, but on God, who richly supplies us with all things to enjoy.
1 TIMOTHY 6:17 NASB

My friend Claire lived large with a millionaire husband, enormous house, designer clothes, and flashy convertible—even a cook (to my envy!). But suddenly, the economy plunged south, and in the twinkle of a bank vault key, she lost it all. Divorced, homeless, and bitter, Claire was forced to wait tables to pay her ill son's medical bills. We can't depend on money—here today, gone tomorrow. Our hope must be fixed on our eternal God.

MORNING
Every Knee Will Bow

It is written: "'As surely as I live,' says the Lord, 'every knee
will bow before me; every tongue will acknowledge God.'"
ROMANS 14:11 NIV

Can you imagine what it will be like on that day when every
knee bows and every tongue confesses that Jesus Christ is Lord?
Oh, what joy that will be! May our love for God and our love for
His people motivate us to reach the unreached people groups of
the world. Every day we're one step closer to that glorious day!

EVENING
Seeking After Love

Whoever covers an offense seeks love,
but he who repeats a matter separates close friends.
PROVERBS 17:9 ESV

We don't get to pick our family members, but we can select our friends.
And when we do, we're making a love pact with them. In essence, we're
saying: "We're in this for the long haul. We will forgive quickly, love
deeply, and keep our conversations private." Good friends seek after
love, even when times get tough. *Especially* when times get tough.

MORNING

Dwelling in Joy

Surely the righteous will praise your name
and the upright will live in your presence.
PSALM 140:13 NIV

Have you ever gone camping in a tent? What if you had a special place
a quiet, private place like that tent where you could dwell with God?
A private place of worship? Wouldn't you want to linger inside that
holy habitat, separating yourself from the outside world? Pitch your
tent today. . .and spend some time inside with the King of kings.

EVENING

Only the Best

I have hidden your word in my heart
that I might not sin against you.
PSALM 119:11 NLT

Memorizing scripture is like preparing chicken salad for the soul.
God's Word (quality ingredients) will be ready at a moment's notice
to guide, comfort, and train us in righteousness (quality results).
Anything else is just gizzards.

MORNING
No Division

In Christ's family there can be no division into Jew and non-Jew,
slave and free, male and female. Among us you are all equal.
GALATIANS 3:28 MSG

Grace is a gift that none of us deserve—and by grace Jesus has removed
all barriers between God and ourselves. God asks that as members of His
family we also knock down all the walls we've built between ourselves
and others. Not just the obvious ones, but also the ones that may hide
in our blind spots. In Christ, there is no liberal or conservative,
no educated or uneducated, no division whatsoever.

EVENING
Joy-Scatterers

Light-seeds are planted in the souls of God's people,
Joy-seeds are planted in good heart-soil.
PSALM 97:11 MSG

Imagine a farmer dropping seeds into fertile soil. They're sure to spring
up. That's how it is with joy. Keep it with you at all times, like seeds in
your pocket. Then, when you find fertile soil in the workplace, at the
doctor's office, around the dinner table pull out a few of those seeds
and sprinkle them around. Oh, the joy that will spring forth!

By This All People Will Know

"A new commandment I give to you, that you love one another: just as I have loved you, you also are to love one another. By this all people will know that you are my disciples, if you have love for one another."
JOHN 13:34–35 ESV

The Bible says that people will know we're God's kids by our love. Love itself is our greatest witness. It's even more important than sharing the Gospel or laying out the four spiritual laws. Those things are important, but love is still the key. We back up our words with our actions. And when we love others—truly love them—our words are much more palatable.

Priorities

Let all that you do be done in love.
1 CORINTHIANS 16:14 NASB

Sometimes we get so wrapped up in our daily to-do lists that we put our duties above people. "Leave me alone until this project is finished, kids." "Sorry, Sue, I'm too busy to have lunch." "Oh, I don't have time to talk to Mom today; I'll let the answering machine get it." How, then, can we ever share the love of Christ with those we've shoved out of our way? People don't care how much you know until they know how much you care.

MORNING
A Happy Heart

*Therefore my heart is glad and my glory [my inner self] rejoices;
my body too shall rest and confidently dwell in safety.*
PSALM 16:9 AMP

Ever wish you could take a day off? Feel like you're always running
full-steam ahead? The Lord designed our bodies to require rest, and if
we skip that part of the equation, we suffer the consequences! If you
want your body to "confidently dwell in safety," then you must get the
rest you need. Rest makes for a happy heart. . .and a healthy body.

EVENING
Love Covers All Wrongs

*"For this reason I say to you, her sins, which are many, have been forgiven,
for she loved much; but he who is forgiven little, loves little."*
LUKE 7:47 NASB

If you've ever been forgiven for something you considered really
grievous, then you know what it means to be grateful! Love covers
all wrongs. It also forgives on a grand scale. To extend this kind of
forgiveness, you have to genuinely love the other person,
both in word and deed. Love big. Forgive big.

MORNING
Back to God

My dear brothers and sisters, always be willing to listen and slow to speak.
Do not become angry easily, because anger will not
help you live the right kind of life God wants.
JAMES 1:19–20 NCV

Our feelings are gifts from God, and we should never be ashamed
of them. Instead, we need to offer them all back to God, both our
joys and our frustrations. When we give God our anger,
our irritation, our hurt feelings, and our frustrations, we make
room in our hearts to truly hear what others are saying.

EVENING
Pebbles

I will give you a new heart and put a new spirit within you, and I will
remove the heart of stone from your flesh, and give you a heart of flesh.
EZEKIEL 36:26 NASB

So many things can harden our hearts: overwhelming loss,
shattered dreams; even scar tissue from broken hearts, disillusionment,
and disappointment. To avoid pain, we simply turn off feelings.
Our hearts become petrified rock—heavy, cold, and rigid. But God
can crack our hearts of stone from the inside out and replace that
miserable pile of pebbles with soft, feeling hearts of flesh.
The amazing result is a brand-new, hope-filled spirit.

MORNING

Singing of His Love

I will sing of the LORD's great love forever; with my mouth I will make your faithfulness known through all generations. I will declare that your love stands firm forever, that you have established your faithfulness in heaven itself.

PSALM 89:1–2 NIV

When you're filled with the love of the Lord, it's hard to contain the song that rises up in your heart. Why stop it? Let it flow! Praise makes even the hardest situation manageable. And what a great witness! When others hear you humming, when they see your passion for praise, they will wonder what you have that they don't. Join in the great love song of all time today—praise to the King of kings!

EVENING

Joyful Patience

Strengthened with all might, according to his glorious power, unto all patience and longsuffering with joyfulness.

COLOSSIANS 1:11 KJV

You've heard the old adage, "Don't pray for patience! God will surely give you a reason to need it!" Here's the truth: As you wait on the Lord, He promises to strengthen you with all might, according to His glorious power. So, what's a little waiting, as long as God is giving you strength? And you know where that strength comes from after all. . .the joy of the Lord *is* your strength!

MORNING
A Sacrifice of Praise

Is any among you afflicted? let him pray.
Is any merry? let him sing psalms.
JAMES 5:13 KJV

It's tough to praise when you're not feeling well, isn't it? But that's exactly what God calls us to do. If you're struggling today, reach way down deep. . . . Out of your pain, your weakness, offer God a sacrifice of praise. Spend serious time in prayer. Lift up a song of joy even if it's a weak song! You'll be surprised how He energizes you with His great joy!

EVENING
One Nation under God

The poor are filled with hope, and injustice is silenced.
JOB 5:16 CEV

"Give me your tired, your poor, your huddled masses. . . ." beckons the Statue of Liberty, offering a home and freedom to hurting people. Many of our ancestors flocked to American shores that were offering freedom of worship and an end to the injustice of religious persecution. May we never forget the sacrifices they made to pursue the hope of providing their children—you and me—with a nation founded on Christian principles. Let's strive to preserve that hope for future generations.

MORNING
Perception

"The LORD himself goes before you and will be with you; he will never leave you nor forsake you. Do not be afraid; do not be discouraged."
DEUTERONOMY 31:8 NIV

The world we see with our eyes is only a piece of reality, a glimpse into an enormous and mysterious universe. Just as our eyes often deceive us, so do our feelings. We perceive life through our emotions, but they are as limited as our physical vision. Whether we sense God's presence or not, He is always with us. Grace waits to meet us in the future, so we can disregard all our feelings of fear and discouragement.

EVENING
Prosperous Love

Love prospers when a fault is forgiven,
but dwelling on it separates close friends.
PROVERBS 17:9 NLT

When we forgive someone who's wronged us, we're offering proof of our love. No, forgiving doesn't always mean reconciliation. Sometimes we need to separate for a season. Forgiveness doesn't imply an ongoing close relationship. God often calls friends and loved ones to take a sabbatical from each other. But love and forgiveness are still in order, even in the toughest situations.

MORNING

Directed by Love

*May the Lord direct your hearts into the love
of God and into the steadfastness of Christ.*
2 THESSALONIANS 3:5 NASB

It's interesting to read that God occasionally needs to direct our hearts into His love. Think about how you steer a car. The steering wheel needs a little nudge to the right or the left. That's how it is with love, too. If we don't willingly accept God's little nudges, our love for others can grow cold. Keep your witness strong by allowing the Lord to direct your heart as He sees fit.

EVENING

Do a Little Dance

*Then Miriam the prophet, Aaron's sister, took a tambourine
and led all the women as they played their tambourines and danced.*
EXODUS 15:20 NLT

Can you imagine the enormous celebration that broke out among the children of Israel when God miraculously saved them from Pharaoh's army at the Red Sea? Even dignified prophetess Miriam grabbed her tambourine and cut loose with her girlfriends. Despite adverse circumstances, she heard God's music and did His dance. Isn't that our goal today? To Hear God's music above the world's cacophony and do His dance as we recognize everyday miracles in our lives?

Morning
Be of Good Cheer

A cheerful disposition is good for your health;
gloom and doom leave you bone-tired.
PROVERBS 17:22 MSG

Want to stay in the best possible health? Do you take vitamins every day? Eat right? Exercise? Here's one more thing you can add to your daily regimen for good health, a prescription for long life: cheerfulness. Yes, that's right! To ward off disease, try joy. According to the proverb above, it's the very flower of health. And it's just what the doctor ordered.

Evening
The Path of Joy

Moses spoke to the people: "Don't be afraid. Stand firm
and watch GOD do his work of salvation for you today."
EXODUS 14:13 MSG

When we're waiting on a miracle, the minutes seem to drag by. We force our attentions ahead to tomorrow. . .in the hopes that we'll receive the answer we long for. But what about today? This is the day the Lord has made! He wants us to rejoice in it. So what if the answer hasn't come yet? So what if patience is required? Don't miss the opportunity to connect with God. . .today!

MORNING
Letting Go

A peaceful heart leads to a healthy body;
jealousy is like cancer in the bones.
PROVERBS 14:30 NLT

Some emotions are meant to be nourished, and others need to be quickly dropped into God's hands. Learn to cultivate and seek out that which brings peace to your heart. And practice letting go of your negative feelings as quickly as you can, releasing them to God. If you cling to these dark feelings, they will reproduce like a cancer, blocking the healthy flow of grace into your life.

EVENING
24/7

He will not let your foot slip—
he who watches over you will not slumber.
PSALM 121:3 NIV

I love hiking the winding mountain paths near our remote Smoky Mountain cabin. Sometimes I get so caught up in watching hummingbirds or admiring cliff-side vistas that I stumble, forgetting that inattention could be deadly. How comforting to know that our Lord is always alert as He watches over us. We don't have to worry that an important prayer will slip by while He sneezes or that He'll nap through our surgery. He's always on duty.

MORNING
The One I Love

"Here is my servant whom I have chosen, the one I love, in whom I delight;
I will put my Spirit on him, and he will proclaim justice to the nations."
MATTHEW 12:18 NIV

It's easier to be a good witness when we realize that God has given us
His Spirit. It also helps to know that we're loved whether we mess up or
not. And we do mess up, don't we! We set out to share God's love with
a friend and end up in an argument with her instead. Ugh! Still, God
loves us, and His Spirit gives us the courage to go out and try again.

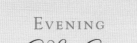

EVENING
A Love Song

By day the LORD directs his love, at night his
song is with me—a prayer to the God of my life.
PSALM 42:8 NIV

Nighttime prayers are so precious. Our last words to God before
our head hits the pillow stir our hearts to praise through the night.
And what a wonderful gift prayer is. It's an awesome privilege.
We get to communicate with the Creator of all! We share our hurts,
our pains, our joys, and our questions. Then the Lord responds
by speaking to us, whispering words of love and direction.

MORNING

Joyous Hope

May the God of hope fill you with all joy and peace as you trust in him,
so that you may overflow with hope by the power of the Holy Spirit.
ROMANS 15:13 NIV

Isn't it fun to think about God pouring joy into our lives?
Imagine yourself with a water pitcher in hand, pouring out, out,
out. . .covering everything in sight. The Lord wants us, through
the power of the Spirit, to overflow. To bubble over. To experience
not just joy, but hope—a benefit of joy. Today, as you spend time
in prayer, allow God to saturate you with His joyous hope.

EVENING

Joy in Place of Tears

They that sow in tears shall reap in joy.
PSALM 126:5 KJV

Periods of great sorrow are unavoidable. Perhaps the death of a loved
one has left you floundering. Or maybe your heart has been broken by
someone you thought you could trust. If you've been through an earthshaking change—one you weren't expecting or feel you didn't deserve—
then turn to the One who can replenish you. God will walk with you
through this valley and promises to replace your tears with joy.

MORNING
True Nourishment

He gives food to every living thing.
His faithful love endures forever.
PSALM 136:25 NLT

People often have a confused relationship with food. We love to eat,
but we feel guilty when we do. We sometimes turn to food when we're
tense or worried, trying to fill the empty, anxious holes in our hearts.
But God wants to give us the true nourishment we need,
body and soul, if only we will let Him.

EVENING
Answered Prayers

But the angel said to him, "Do not be afraid, Zacharias,
for your prayer is heard; and your wife Elizabeth will bear you a son,
and you shall call his name John."
LUKE 1:13 NKJV

Zacharias, though quite old, had been praying for a child for years.
How funny that the angel prepared him by saying, "Don't be afraid,"
before sharing the news! This answered prayer, though joyous,
surely rocked Zacharias and Elizabeth's world! Have you ever
consistently prayed for something without getting the answer you
want? Ever felt like giving up? Don't! When you least expect it,
your answer could come. . .and it just might rock your world!

MORNING
Loving Those in Need

If anyone has material possessions and sees a brother or sister in need but has no pity on them, how can the love of God be in that person?
1 JOHN 3:17 NIV

If we love God, we need to take care of others even if it means reaching into our wallet to do it. Material possessions are meant to be shared. They're a tool for ministering to others. People see our love when we take pity on them in their need. And when we give, our hearts are exposed. Love comes pouring out.

EVENING
One Gutsy Gal

It could be that you were made queen for a time like this!
ESTHER 4:14 CEV

Crowned queen after winning a beauty contest, Esther was only allowed audience with her king when summoned. A wave of his scepter would pardon her from execution, but he was a hard man— and unpredictable. When Esther learned of a plot to destroy her people, she faced a tough decision. She was the *only* one who could save them— at supreme risk. God had intentionally placed her in that position for that time. What's your divinely ordained position?

MORNING
Our Hope, Our Joy

For what is our hope, or joy, or crown of rejoicing? Is it not even you in the presence of our Lord Jesus Christ at His coming?
1 THESSALONIANS 2:19 NKJV

Isn't it funny how the words *hope* and *joy* just seem to fit together? You rarely find one without the other. If you have hope in the unseen tomorrow, then joy rises up in your soul to give you strength for the journey. Spend time in God's holy presence today. In that place, you will find both hope. . .and joy.

EVENING
Extending Love and Prayer

"But I tell you, love your enemies and pray for those who persecute you."
MATTHEW 5:44 NIV

We usually enjoy praying for others, as long as we're in good relationship with them. But this whole "Pray for your enemies" thing is tough! We don't want to ask God to bless our enemies. If we're honest, we're usually hoping for the opposite! But God commands us to love our enemies and to pray for them, too. So who's on your "enemy" list today? Better get busy!

MORNING
Daily Miracles

"That is why I tell you not to worry about everyday life—whether you have enough food and drink, or enough clothes to wear. Isn't life more than food, and your body more than clothing?"
MATTHEW 6:25 NLT

With our eyes fixed on what we *don't* have, we often overlook the grace we have already received. God has blessed us in many ways. Our bodies function day after day in amazing ways we take for granted, and life is filled with an abundance of daily miracles. Why do we worry so much about the details when we live in such a vast sea of daily grace?

EVENING
Deliver Us. . .with Joy!

And lead us not into temptation, but deliver us from evil: For thine is the kingdom, and the power, and the glory, for ever. Amen.
MATTHEW 6:13 KJV

Have you ever been ensnared by the enemy? Led into temptation? Caught in his trap? When you give your heart to Christ, you are set free from your past, delivered from the bondage of sin. Talk about a reason to celebrate. Nothing is more glorious than being led out of a prison cell into the sunlight. Oh, joyous freedom! Today, praise God for the things He has delivered you from.

MORNING
A Fragrant Offering

Christ loved us and gave himself up for us
as a fragrant offering and sacrifice to God.
EPHESIANS 5:2 NIV

If we ever want to know how to give, all we have to do is follow God's example. He gave His only Son so that we would have life. Talk about a fragrant love offering! Giving is sacrificial, which means it isn't always pleasant. We have to remember that giving isn't about us. It's about our love for God and His people. Love is a great motivator to give.

EVENING
Joy Leads the Way

Then will I go unto the altar of God, unto God my exceeding joy:
yea, upon the harp will I praise thee, O God my God.
PSALM 43:4 KJV

We're instructed to come into the Lord's presence with a joy-filled heart. . .to praise our way into the throne room. Perhaps you're not a musician. You don't own an instrument and only sing in the shower. Don't let that keep you from approaching the altar with a song of praise on your lips. Today, let joy lead the way, and may your praises be glorious!

MORNING
Joyous Perspective

*Let us draw near to God with a sincere
heart and with the full assurance that faith brings.*
HEBREWS 10:22 NIV

Ever looked through a pair of binoculars? What if you peered through
the lenses and caught a glimpse of God's face? What if you could see
things the way He sees them? Hear things the way He hears them?
What an amazing perspective! Every time you draw near to God, He
offers you the opportunity to see Him. To find Him. To trust Him. Let
Him give you His joyous perspective today.

EVENING
Cool Summer Shower

*He will renew your life and
sustain you in your old age.*
RUTH 4:15 NIV

Ruth's blessing of renewal is applicable to us today. *Renovatio* is Latin
for "rebirth." It means casting off the old and embracing the new:
a revival of spirit, a renovation of attitude. Something essential for
women to espouse every day of their lives. Like a cool rain shower on
a sizzling summer day, Ruth's hope was renewed by her Lord's touch,
and ours will be, too, if we look to Him for daily replenishing.

MORNING
Dancing in the Puddles

And so, Lord, where do I put my hope?
My only hope is in you.
PSALM 39:7 NLT

They say you can tell a lot about a person's foundation of hope by the
way she handles a rainy day. Does she turn into a gloomy Gussy, wailing
"Oh, woe is me. . ." or does she make the best of a bad situation?
A hope-filled person will realize that abundant life in Christ isn't about
simply enduring the storm but also about learning to dance in the
puddles. So grab your galoshes, and let's boogie!

EVENING
No Love Withheld

Praise be to God, who has not rejected
my prayer or withheld his love from me!
PSALM 66:20 NIV

Sometimes we're afraid to pray because we're upset with the Lord or
others. We're afraid that if we get gut-honest with God in our prayers,
He might reject us. Not so! He will not withhold His love from us, even
when we're mad at Him! He's a big God. He can take it. So get it out.
Confess your angst. Then watch as He sets everything right again,
with His amazing love leading the way!

MORNING
God's Honor

For the honor of your name, O LORD,
forgive my many, many sins.
PSALM 25:11 NLT

Like all gifts of grace, forgiveness by its very definition is nothing that can ever be earned. Forgiveness is what God gives us when we deserve nothing but anger. He forgives us not because we merit it, but because of His own honor. Over and over, we will turn away from God— but over and over, He will bring us back. That is who He is!

EVENING
Thanking Him. . .Publicly!

Give thanks unto the LORD, call upon his name,
make known his deeds among the people.
1 CHRONICLES 16:8 KJV

It's one thing to thank God in the privacy of your prayer closet; it's another to openly talk about the amazing things He's done in your life in front of a watching world. The words of your mouth, lifted up in joyful testimony, could have an amazing impact on those around you. So, go ahead. . .thank Him publicly. Share the things He's done with people you come in contact with. Make His deeds known!

MORNING
Unexpected Joy

*Do not be conformed to this world, but be
transformed by the renewing of your mind.*
ROMANS 12:2 NKJV

Do you ever find yourself worrying about tomorrow? Not sure of what
it will bring? Oh, what hope lies in the unseen tomorrow! What
unexpected joys are just around the corner. Sure, you can't see them. . .
but they're there! Before you give in to fear, allow the Lord to transform
your mind. See tomorrow as He sees it filled with unexpected joys.

EVENING
Hearts Filled with Joy

*"He provides you with plenty of
food and fills your hearts with joy."*
ACTS 14:17 NIV

When we think about provision, we usually think in terms of money,
don't we? Getting the bills paid. Having food in the pantry. Making
sure our needs are met. But what about our emotional needs? Does the
Lord make provision in that area, as well? Of course! According to this
scripture, He fills our hearts with joy. What an awesome God we serve!

MORNING
Walking Faith

Be strong and courageous, and act; do not fear nor be dismayed,
for the LORD God, my God, is with you. He will not fail you nor forsake you.
1 CHRONICLES 28:20 NASB

What a life verse! What a creed to live by! We are assured that our
God will never leave us or forsake us. We draw strength and courage
from this assurance and are then able to *act*; to share our faith
boldly—without fear—because we are never alone. The Lord God—
our God—is with us.

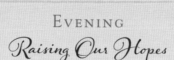

EVENING
Raising Our Hopes

"Did I ask you for a son, my lord?" she said.
"Didn't I tell you, 'Don't raise my hopes'?"
2 KINGS 4:28 NIV

Are you afraid to raise your hope in God's provision for fear that
hope will crash and burn? The woman from Shunem had everything
but her heart's desire—a child. She was afraid to believe Elisha's
prediction of her pregnancy, but his prayerful intervention made her
dream come true. When the boy later died, however, she lashed out.
God restored her son and raised her hope from the dead. Literally.
Dare we raise our hopes, too?

Morning
Wholly and Completely

"Forgive others, and you will be forgiven."
Luke 6:37 nlt

The words *forgive* and *pardon* come from very old words that mean
"to give up completely and wholeheartedly." When we forgive others,
we totally give up our rights to feel we've been injured or slighted.
And in return, God's grace totally fills the gaps left behind when
we let go of our own selfishness. As we give ourselves wholeheartedly
to others, God gives Himself completely to us.

Evening
A Confession of Love

I prayed to the Lord my God and confessed:
"Lord, the great and awesome God, who keeps his covenant
of love with those who love him and keep his commands."
Daniel 9:4 niv

Prayer is such a wonderful gift. We get to talk to the King of kings and
Lord of lords—and He responds! Our prayer time is also a wonderful
time to thank God for His great love toward us. Why not spend some
time praising Him today? Climb up into His lap and lean your head
against His chest. Make a confession of your love for your Daddy, God.

Morning
Joy. . .in Spite of. . .

"Until now you have not asked for anything in my name.
Ask and you will receive, and your joy will be complete."
JOHN 16:24 NIV

Have you ever faced a truly impossible situation? One so extreme
that, unless God moved, everything else would surely crumble?
God is a God of the impossible. And He wants us to ask, even when
we're facing insurmountable obstacles. In fact, He wants us to know
that only He can perform miracles. Our job? We're called to trust
Him. Then, when those impossible situations turn around,
our "joy tank" will be completely filled to overflowing!

Evening
Wisdom. . .What Joy!

Happy is the man who finds wisdom,
and the man who gains understanding.
PROVERBS 3:13 NKJV

Imagine you've lost a priceless jewel, one passed down from your
grandmother to your mother and then to you. You search everywhere,
under every rock, in every closet. Still, you can't find it. Finally,
in the least likely spot. . .you discover it! Joy floods your soul!
Now imagine that "jewel" is wisdom. You've stumbled across it,
and oh, what a treasure! Talk about a happy find!

MORNING
Interior Decorator

You, O LORD, are a shield about me,
my glory, and the One who lifts my head.
PSALM 3:3 NASB

Have you ever caught a glimpse of yourself reflected in a window and were shocked at the hangdog image you unwittingly portrayed? Slumped shoulders, drooping head, defeated expression? You can straighten your posture and adjust your face, but if the change doesn't come from the inside out, it won't stick. God is our Interior Decorator. Only He can provide that inner joy that projects outward and lifts our heads. Invite Him in to work on your place.

EVENING
Wells of Salvation

With joy you will drink deeply
from the fountain of salvation!
ISAIAH 12:3 NLT

In biblical times, women would go to the local well for water. They would drop the bucket down, down, down, then lift it up, filled to the brim. Today, the Lord wants you to reach down into His well of salvation and, with great joy, draw up the bucket. Remember how He saved you? Delivered you? Remember His grace? Is your bucket filled to the brim? If so, then that's something to celebrate!

MORNING
Brought Forth with Joy

And he brought forth his people with joy,
and his chosen with gladness.
PSALM 105:43 KJV

Have you ever been delivered out of a terrible situation? Lifted out of it, unharmed? Were you stunned when it happened? Had you given up? God is in the deliverance business! And when He lifts us out of impossible situations, we are overwhelmed with joy. . .and we're surprised! Why do we doubt His goodness? The next time you're in a tough spot, expect to be "brought forth with joy."

EVENING
Zombie Zone

Be joyful in hope, patient in affliction,
faithful in prayer.
ROMANS 12:12 NIV

Affliction has a tendency to suck the joy right out of our lives, leaving us stranded in the dully-funks. You know—that black hole of existence where our minds fog, emotions go numb, eyes glaze over, and we languish in a state of spiritual dullness. A spiritual zombie zone. But if we're faithful in prayer, God will be faithful to rescue us from those joy-sucking dully-funks and fill us to the brim with His abundant joy.

MORNING
Lavish and Abundant

Let them come back to GOD, who is merciful,
come back to our God, who is lavish with forgiveness.
ISAIAH 55:7 MSG

God's forgiveness is never stingy or grudging. And He never waits to offer it to us. Instead, it's always there, a lavish, abundant flood of grace, just waiting for us to turn away from our sin and accept it.

EVENING
No Fear in Love

There is no fear in love. But perfect love drives out fear, because fear has
to do with punishment. The one who fears is not made perfect in love.
1 JOHN 4:18 NIV

Oh, what a joy to know that love conquers fear. Think about that for a moment. When fear grips your heart, telling you that you're going to fail at something, God's love drives out that fear. It sends a calming message, one you can rest in. Next time fear slips in, remember it's not from God. He extends perfect love, the only force powerful enough to drive out fear!

MORNING
Inside-Out Love

God has made everything beautiful for its own time.
ECCLESIASTES 3:11 NLT

Beauty is a concern of every woman to some degree. We worry about hair, makeup, weight, fashions. But real beauty can come only from God's inside-out love. Once we are able to finally comprehend His infinite and extravagant love for us—despite our flat feet and split ends—our heart-glow will reflect radiant beauty from the inside out. Only when we feel truly loved are we free to be truly lovely.

EVENING
Walking Uprightly

Folly is joy to him who is destitute of discernment,
but a man of understanding walks uprightly.
PROVERBS 15:21 NKJV

Ever noticed that people who have something to hide don't look others in the eye? Their gaze shifts up, down, and all around. But those who walk uprightly can look others in the eye without guilt or shame. Live wisely. Hold your head high. Look folks in the eye. Let wisdom lead the way and watch as joy follows!

MORNING
The Joy of the Lord Is Your Strength

"This day is holy to our Lord. Do not grieve,
for the joy of the LORD is your strength."
NEHEMIAH 8:10 NIV

Is it possible to have joy in the middle of catastrophic circumstances? What if you're facing the loss of a job? A devastating illness? The death of a loved one? Can you really look beyond your grief to find the joy? Our very strength comes from the joy God places inside us, and we need that strength even more when we're facing seemingly impossible odds! Today, may God's joy strengthen you from the inside out.

EVENING
He's Waiting. . .

"The eyes of the LORD watch over those who do right,
and his ears are open to their prayers."
1 PETER 3:12 NLT

You don't have to try to get God's attention. He is watching you right now. His ear is tuned to your voice. All you need to do is speak, and He will hear you. Receive the gift of grace He gives to you through prayer. Tell God your thoughts, your feelings, your hopes, your joys. He's waiting to listen to you.

MORNING

Everyday Blessings

But the eyes of the LORD are on those who fear him,
on those whose hope is in his unfailing love.
PSALM 33:18 NIV

The Lord of all creation is watching our every moment and
wants to fill us with His joy. He often interrupts our lives with His
blessings: butterflies dancing in sunbeams, dew-touched spiderwebs,
cotton candy clouds, and glorious crimson sunsets. The beauty of His
creation reassures us of His unfailing love and fills us with hope.
But it is up to us to take the time to notice.

EVENING

Divine Refreshment

You were tired out by the length of your road, yet you did not say,
"It is hopeless." You found renewed strength, therefore you did not faint.
ISAIAH 57:10 NASB

By the end of each day, most women are ready to collapse. Tight
schedules, relentless deadlines, and plaguing debts make our daily roads
not just physically tiring but spiritually draining. Our reserves border
on empty. How encouraging to know that renewed strength is available
through the fountain that never runs dry. If we fill our buckets with
living water—Bible reading, Christian music, inspirational books and
DVDs—we will not faint, but enjoy divine refreshment.

MORNING
Unconditional Grace

A friend loves at all times.
PROVERBS 17:17 NASB

Friends are the people you can allow to see you at your worst. They're the ones who can see you without your makeup. . .or walk in when your house is a mess. . .or overhear you acting like a thirteen-year-old—and they'll still be your friends. They reveal to you God's unconditional grace.

EVENING
Quieted by Love

"The LORD your God is with you, the Mighty Warrior who saves.
He will take great delight in you, in his love he will no longer rebuke you,
but will rejoice over you with singing."
ZEPHANIAH 3:17 NIV

If you're a parent, you know what it's like to rock a baby in your arms, calming him down so that he can sleep. Your words of love—sweetly sung—can quiet even the loudest squall. It's the same when we climb into God's arms. He quiets us with His love, calms our fears, and dries our eyes. We drift off to sleep with His gentle words of love drifting over us.

MORNING
Exceeding Joy

But rejoice, inasmuch as ye are partakers of Christ's sufferings; that, when his glory shall be revealed, ye may be glad also with exceeding joy.
1 PETER 4:13 KJV

We want to know Christ both in the glory of His resurrection and in the fellowship of His sufferings. If we're open to really knowing Him in both ways, then we've got to be vulnerable. Finding a balance is key. It really is possible to go through times of suffering and still maintain your joy. After all, joy is a choice.

EVENING
A Witness to the Nations

"Go therefore and make disciples of all the nations."
MATTHEW 28:19 NASB

Have you ever pondered the mandate in Matthew's Gospel to go into all the world and preach the Gospel? Ever feel like you're not doing your part? God calls us to be witnesses where we are to bloom where we're planted. Imagine the joy of leading a neighbor or a friend to the Lord. So, instead of fretting over not doing enough, delight in the fact that you are useable. . .right where you are.

MORNING
Our Companion

Our LORD, you are the friend of your worshipers,
and you make an agreement with all of us.
PSALM 25:14 CEV

God is our Friend. He is our companion through life's journey;
He is the One who always understands us; and no matter what
we do, He always accepts us and loves us. What better agreement
could we ever have with anyone than what we have with God?

EVENING
Right Now

For God says, "At just the right time, I heard you. On the day of salvation,
I helped you." Indeed, the "right time" is now. Today is the day of salvation.
2 CORINTHIANS 6:2 NLT

God always meets us right now, in the present moment.
We don't need to waste our time looking over our shoulders at
the past, and we don't have to feel as though we need to reach
some future moment before we can truly touch God. He is here now.
Today, this very moment, is full of His grace.

MORNING
My Refuge

God is our refuge and strength,
always ready to help in times of trouble.
PSALM 46:1 NLT

What is your quiet place? The place you go to get away from the fray, to chill out, think, regroup, and gain perspective? Mine is a hammock nestled beneath a canopy of oaks in my backyard. . .nobody around but birds, squirrels, an occasional wasp, God, and me. There I can pour out my heart to my Lord, *hear* His comforting voice, and *feel* His strength refresh me. We all need a quiet place. God, our refuge, will meet us there.

EVENING
Nonstick Attitudes

A joyful heart is good medicine.
PROVERBS 17:22 NASB

Laughter is to hope as nonstick cooking spray is to a shiny new muffin tin: it keeps the goo from sticking. Once the batter of everyday responsibility hardens and adheres to our attitudes, it's awfully hard to scrape off enough crust for hope to shine through. But if we coat our day with a little laughter and the joy of the Lord, problems will slide off a lot better. And hope sparkles.

MORNING
Make a Joyful Noise

O come, let us sing unto the LORD:
let us make a joyful noise to the rock of our salvation.
PSALM 95:1 KJV

Do you love to sing praises to God? Perhaps your voice isn't the best. Maybe you can't carry a tune in a bucket, but you long to praise God anyway. Go ahead and do it! We're told in scripture to "make a joyful noise" to the Lord. We're not told it has to be with a trained voice. So, lift up those praises! He accepts them, on key or off!

EVENING
Love Overcomes Timidity

For the spirit God gave us does not make us timid,
but gives us power, love and self-discipline.
2 TIMOTHY 1:7 NIV

Sometimes we're afraid to share our testimony with others or to talk about our faith. We're timid. We hold back. How wonderful to realize that God gave us a spirit of power, love, and self-discipline. With these three things firmly in place, we're able to open up and share the good news of His love.

MORNING
Redeeming Pain

I may have fallen, but I will get up;
I may be sitting in the dark, but the LORD is my light.
MICAH 7:8 CEV

"Life *is* pain, Highness. Anyone who says differently is selling something." This memorable line from the movie, *The Princess Bride*, rings true. Pain is inevitable in life, but God can use it for redemptive purposes. Pain can knock us down, cast us into darkness, and make us feel defeated. But it's only as debilitating as we allow it to be. We *will* get up again; we *will* learn, adapt, and grow through redeeming pain.

EVENING
Powerful Witnesses

"But you will receive power when the Holy Spirit has come upon you;
and you shall be My witnesses both in Jerusalem, and in all Judea and
Samaria, and even to the remotest part of the earth."
ACTS 1:8 NASB

Want to experience real joy in your life? Then become a powerful witness. The most effective witness for Christ is one who is wholly surrendered to God's will, and who has invited the Holy Spirit to do a transforming work in her life. After all, we can't really share the good news if our lives haven't been truly changed. Allow the Lord to renovate you from the inside out then change your world!

MORNING
Never Failing. . .

My friends scorn me,
but I pour out my tears to God.
JOB 16:20 NLT

Sometimes even the best friends can let you down. Human beings
aren't perfect. But God's grace will never fail you. When even
your closest friends don't understand you, take your hurt to Him.

EVENING
See Jesus

God left nothing that is not subject to them. Yet at present
we do not see everything subject to them. But we do see Jesus.
HEBREWS 2:8–9 NIV

We know that Jesus has won the victory over sin, and yet when we
look at the world as it is right now, we still see sin all around us.
We see pain and suffering, greed and selfishness, brokenness and despair.
We know that the world is not ruled by God. Yet despite that, we can
look past the darkness of sin. By grace, right now, we can see Jesus.

Morning

Joyful in Glory

Let the saints be joyful in glory:
let them sing aloud upon their beds.
PSALM 149:5 KJV

When do you like to spend time alone with the Lord?
In the morning, as the stillness of the day sweeps over you?
At night, when you rest your head upon the pillow? Start your
conversation with praise. Let your favorite worship song or hymn
pour forth! Tell Him how blessed you are to be His child. This private
praise time will strengthen you and will fill your heart with joy!

Evening

Two-Stranded Rope

The widow who is really in need and left all alone puts her hope in
God and continues night and day to pray and to ask God for help.
1 TIMOTHY 5:5 NIV

Some women feel as though they are irreparably weakened when they
are widowed. Where there once were three strands of a sturdy rope (his,
hers, and God's), there now are two. But those who persevere through
faith and true grit say the secret is to learn to rejoice in what's left instead
of lamenting what has been lost. Look forward. Move forward. Keep that
two-stranded rope strong, and never lose hope of a better tomorrow.

MORNING
See Ya, Self

Blessed are the poor in spirit,
for theirs is the kingdom of heaven.
MATTHEW 5:3 NASB

We don't often think of ourselves as "poor in spirit," but this passage refers to those who are not full of themselves; those who are filled instead with God's spirit. "Poor" in this context means *selfless* rather than *selfish*; those with an attitude of dependence on God. How do we become poor in spirit and revel in the hope and promise of heaven? By emptying ourselves of *self* and the pride of self-sufficiency, and refilling ourselves with Jesus.

EVENING
Stouthearted Love

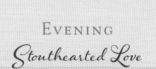

When I called, you answered me;
you greatly emboldened me.
PSALM 138:3 NIV

Love doesn't cower in fear. It holds its head up high and smiles in the face of a challenge. It cries out, "Be bold! Be strong!" If you're facing a fearful situation, call out to God. He will answer you and will give you the boldness you need to get through whatever situation you're facing.

MORNING
What You Crave

Take delight in the LORD,
and he will give you your heart's desires.
PSALM 37:4 NLT

Do you ever feel as though God wants to deny you what you want, as though He's a cruel stepparent who takes pleasure in thwarting you? That image of God is a lie. He's the One who placed your heart's desires deep inside you. As you turn to Him, knowing that He alone is the source of all true delight, He will grant you what your heart most truly craves.

EVENING
Bearing Witness

The life appeared; we have seen it and testify to it, and we proclaim to you the eternal life, which was with the Father and has appeared to us.
1 JOHN 1:2 NIV

We don't have to work hard at being good witnesses when we're walking in close relationship with the Lord. Our witness will flow quite naturally out of our relationship with God. In other words, we "are" witnesses, simply by living the life He's called us to live. And by living the life, we point others toward eternal life. Now, that will cause joy to rise up in your soul!

MORNING
With Thanksgiving

I will praise the name of God with a song,
and will magnify him with thanksgiving.
PSALM 69:30 KJV

It's one thing to spend time with God; it's another to praise Him
with a thankful heart. Sometimes we forget His many blessings.
We praise out of routine. Today, allow God to remind you of all
the many ways He has blessed you. Oh, what full and thankful
hearts we have, when we pause to remember. Now, watch your
praises rise to the surface, like cream to the top of the pitcher.

EVENING
The Present Moment

"This day is holy to our Lord."
NEHEMIAH 8:10 NIV

Sometimes we're in such a hurry to get to the future that
we miss out on the present. God has gifts He wants to
give you right now. Don't be so excited about tomorrow
that you overlook the grace He's giving you today.

MORNING
It'll Be All Right

Our comfort is abundant through Christ.
2 CORINTHIANS 1:5 NASB

As children, there's no greater comfort than running to Mommy or Daddy and hearing, "It'll be all right." As adults, when we're frightened, dismayed, or dispirited, we yearn to run to enveloping arms for the same comfort. Abba Father—Papa God—is waiting with open arms to offer us loving comfort in our times of need. If we listen closely, we'll hear His still, small voice speak to our hearts: "It'll be all right, my child."

EVENING
Glimmering Gold

So in everything, do to others what
you would have them do to you.
MATTHEW 7:12 NIV

The Golden Rule. Most of us were raised with this basic guide to human relations, but sometimes the message gets turned around. Instead, we follow the Nedlog (golden backward) Rule: Don't do for others because they don't do for you. But Jesus didn't say repay in kind; He said pay forward. The actions of others are irrelevant. Regardless of what others do, we should treat them the way we'd like to be treated: with respect and consideration.

Morning
Satisfied

Satisfy us in the morning with your unfailing love,
that we may sing for joy and be glad all our days.
PSALM 90:14 NIV

God wants to fulfill you. He wants you to feel satisfied with life so that you will catch yourself humming or singing his praises all day long. Even when life is hard, He is waiting to comfort you with His unfailing love so that gladness will creep over your heart once more.

Evening
Disciplined by Love

The LORD disciplines those he loves,
as a father the son he delights in.
PROVERBS 3:12 NIV

When we discipline our children, it's because we love them and want the best for them. We're training them to be responsible adults. Same with God. He disciplines us out of love because He wants the very best for us. When we strike out on our own, away from His principles and blessings, He has no choice but to reel us back in. Love always disciplines.

MORNING
A Big Song

Shout for joy to the Lord, all the earth,
burst into jubilant song with music.
PSALM 98:4 NIV

Do you ever feel like you don't have enough words to praise God?
Like your vocabulary is limited? Wish you could throw the lid off and
worship Him with abandon? That's exactly what He longs to do—
spend intimate time with you. Sing a *big* song to the Lord. And prepare
yourself for the inevitable joy that will rise up as you do.

EVENING
Joy in Your Work

Go, eat your food with gladness, and drink your wine with
a joyful heart, for it is now that God favors what you do.
ECCLESIASTES 9:7 NIV

Ever feel like nothing you do is good enough?
Your boss is frustrated over something you've done wrong.
The kids are complaining. Your neighbors are even upset at you.
How wonderful to read that God accepts our works, even when
we feel lacking. He encourages us to go our way with a merry heart,
completely confident that we are accepted in the Beloved.

MORNING
I Am His

My health may fail, and my spirit may grow weak,
but God remains the strength of my heart; he is mine forever.
PSALM 73:26 NLT

My dear friend was dying of an inoperable brain tumor. Mother of three, 48-year-old Sherill could no longer walk or care for herself, yet her voice was filled with hope as she gazed unwaveringly into my eyes and quoted this verse. She added something very significant at the end that I'll hold close to my heart and draw strength from when my time comes: "He is mine forever. . .*and I am His.*"

EVENING
Constant Grace

For Jesus doesn't change—yesterday, today,
tomorrow, he's always totally himself.
HEBREWS 13:8 MSG

As human beings, we live in the stream of time. Sometimes all the changes time brings terrify us; sometimes they fill us with joy and excitement. Either way, we can cling to the still point that lies in the middle of our changing world: Jesus Christ, who never changes. His constant grace leads us through all life's changes, and one day it will bring us to our home in heaven, beyond time, where we will be like Him.

MORNING

Expressions of Grace

*So I decided there is nothing better than to enjoy food and drink
and to find satisfaction in work. Then I realized that these
pleasures are from the hand of God.*
ECCLESIASTES 2:24 NLT

Hedonists are people who have decided that life's only meaning lies
in physical pleasures. But they can't escape God's hand. Our food, our
drink, the satisfaction we take in our work, and all the physical pleasures
of our lives are not separate from God. Instead, they are expressions of
His grace. He longs for us to be fulfilled in every way possible.

EVENING

Bet the Farm

*Whoever plows and threshes should be able
to do so in the hope of sharing in the harvest.*
1 CORINTHIANS 9:10 NIV

There's a young man who works in children's church with me who is
loud, brash, impulsive, an incessant talker, and loves the Lord with all
his heart. The kids think he's hilarious. I think he's obnoxious. But I
must remind myself that God uses him in unique ways to reach young
hearts with the Gospel that I never could. He's a plowman and I'm a
thresher, and we work together to harvest souls into God's kingdom.

MORNING
The Joyful Sound

Blessed is the people that know the joyful sound:
they shall walk, O LORD, in the light of thy countenance.
PSALM 89:15 KJV

Imagine a dimly lit room. You can barely make out the shapes of things around you. Somewhere in that room, your Father is waiting for you. Suddenly His voice rings out and joyous relief floods your soul. Even though you cannot see where you are going, the sound of His voice guides you directly into His arms. Allow yourself to tune in to that precious voice today.

EVENING
Tough Love

Love does not delight in evil
but rejoices with the truth.
1 CORINTHIANS 13:6 NIV

It's so hard to watch someone you love get caught up in a sinful lifestyle—for instance, your teen is on drugs or your spouse turns to alcohol. For the first time, your love toward that person changes slightly. It toughens up. It gets a backbone. It says, "This far and no further." And it holds the other person accountable. Tough love. God's all for it. You will be, too, once you've seen its results.

MORNING
Increasing Visibility

Where then is my hope?
JOB 17:15 NIV

On hectic days when fatigue takes its toll, when we feel like cornless husks, hope disappears. When hurting people hurt people and we're in the line of fire, hope vanishes. When ideas fizzle, efforts fail; when we throw the spaghetti against the wall and nothing sticks, hope seems lost. But we must remember it's only temporary. The mountaintop isn't gone just because it's obscured by fog. Visibility will improve tomorrow and hope will rise.

EVENING
A Love That Reaches to the Heavens

Your love, LORD, reaches to the heavens,
your faithfulness to the skies.
PSALM 36:5 NIV

Isn't it interesting to picture God's love sweeping over all of humanity? From His throne in heaven, He pours out this marvelous fountain of love. And with His arms spread wide on the cross, it flowed as a sacrifice for all. His love reaches us when we're in the low places and chases after us when we're in seasons of rebellion. Praise God for His sweeping love!

MORNING
Wonderful Plans

"For I know the plans I have for you," says the LORD. "They are
plans for good and not for disaster, to give you a future and a hope."
JEREMIAH 29:11 NLT

Don't worry about the future. No matter how frightening
it may look to you sometimes, God is waiting there for you.
He has plans for you, wonderful plans that will lead you
deeper and deeper into His grace and love.

EVENING
A Quiet Pace

"Teach me, and I will be quiet.
Show me where I have been wrong."
JOB 6:24 NCV

Do you ever feel as though you simply can't sit still? That your thoughts
are swirling so fast that you can't stop them? That you're so busy,
so stressed, so hurried that you have to run, run, run? Take a breath.
Open your heart to God. Allow Him to quiet your frantic mind.
Ask Him to show you how you can begin again, this time
walking to the quiet pace of His grace.

MORNING

Satisfied by Joy

Satisfy us in the morning with your unfailing love,
that we may sing for joy and be glad all our days.
PSALM 90:14 NIV

You've heard the adage, "You're only as old as you feel." One thing that ages us too quickly is discouragement. We get down and it's hard to get back up again. We need to make a conscious effort each morning to reach out to God. . .to ask Him to satisfy us with His mercy, His loving-kindness. If we're truly satisfied, joy will come. And joy is the best antiwrinkle cream on the market.

EVENING

The Salvage Master

We are pressed on every side by troubles, but we are not crushed.
We are perplexed, but not driven to despair.
2 CORINTHIANS 4:8 NLT

Many women struggle with depression at some point in their lives: postpartum, kids-partum (empty nest), brain-partum (menopause), and anytime in between. We feel that we are being compressed into a rock-hard cube like the product of a trash compactor. The normal details of life suddenly become perplexing and overwhelming. But God does not abandon us to the garbage dump. He is the Salvage Master and recycles us into sterling images of His glory.

MORNING
Safe

My life is in your hands. Save me from my
enemies and from those who are chasing me.
PSALM 31:15 NCV

Do you ever feel like trouble is chasing you? No matter how fast you run or how you try to hide, it comes relentlessly after you, dogging your footsteps, breathing its hot breath down your neck, robbing you of peace. What's even worse is that it waits for you down the road, as well! Maybe you need to stop running and hiding and instead let yourself drop into God's hands, knowing He will hold your future safe.

EVENING
God's Tough Love

"The LORD is slow to anger, abounding in love and forgiving sin and
rebellion. Yet he does not leave the guilty unpunished; he punishes the
children for the sin of the parents to the third and fourth generation."
NUMBERS 14:18 NIV

God is a loving heavenly Father, but He knows how to implement tough love when the situation calls for it. Take Adam and Eve, for instance. Was there ever a more obvious instance of tough love than kicking them out of the garden when they sinned? Yes, God is the author of love—sweet and tough. He believes in consequences. When the need arises, don't be afraid to follow God's example. Love tough.

MORNING
The Eyes Have It

All of you together are Christ's body,
and each of you is a part of it.
1 CORINTHIANS 12:27 NLT

Just as our bodies are compiled of many parts, each essential for functioning as a whole, the body of Christ is made up of hands, feet, ears, hearts, and minds. We women understand this concept but tend to compare ourselves to others. If we're hands, we wish we were feet. If we're noses, we'd rather be eyes. Sometimes we feel like bunions. But God views us as equally important, none better than another. Even us toenails!

EVENING
Nothing Can Separate Us

In all these things we are more than conquerors through him
who loved us. For I am convinced that neither death nor life,
neither angels nor demons, neither the present nor the future,
nor any powers, neither height nor depth, nor anything else
in all creation, will be able to separate us from the love
of God that is in Christ Jesus our Lord.
ROMANS 8:37–39 NIV

Have you ever felt as if you're unlovable? Here's some great news: nothing you've ever done—no sin you've committed, no wicked thought that's flitted through your brain, no temptation you've fallen into—can separate you from God's love. Even when you feel far removed from Him, He's still there, extending His arms of love.

MORNING
Joy in the Journey

*I press toward the mark for the prize of
the high calling of God in Christ Jesus.*
PHILIPPIANS 3:14 KJV

Ever feel like the journey's too long? Like you're not making progress?
Today, ask the Lord to give you joy as you make your way toward the
goal. Don't fret if things aren't happening as quickly as you want them
to. Keep on pressing toward the mark. Thank Him for the process,
and take time to truly take "joy in the journey."

EVENING
Relax. . .

*But I am calm and quiet, like a baby with its mother.
I am at peace, like a baby with its mother.*
PSALM 131:2 NCV

You know how a baby lies completely limp in her mother's arms,
totally trusting and at peace? That is the attitude you need to practice.
Let yourself relax in God's arms, wrapped in His grace. Life will go
on around you, with all its noise and turmoil. Meanwhile, you are
completely safe, totally secure, without a worry in the world.
Lie back and enjoy the quiet!

MORNING
Lord of the Dance

Remember your promise to me, it is my only hope.
PSALM 119:49 NLT

The Bible contains many promises from God: He will protect us (Proverbs 1:33), comfort us (2 Corinthians 1:5), help in our times of trouble (Psalm 46:1), and encourage us (Isaiah 40:29). The word *encourage* comes from the root phrase "to inspire courage." Like an earthly father encouraging his daughter from backstage as her steps falter during her dance recital, our Papa God wants to inspire courage in us, if we only look to Him.

EVENING
Makeover

Since I was worse than anyone else, God had mercy on me and let me be an example of the endless patience of Christ Jesus.
1 TIMOTHY 1:16 CEV

Saul was a Jesus-hater. He went out of his way to hunt down believers to torture, imprison, and kill. Yet Christ tracked *him* down and confronted him in a blinding light on a dusty road. Saul's past no longer mattered. Previous sins were forgiven and forgotten. He was given a fresh start. A life makeover. We, too, are offered a life makeover. Christ offers to create a beautiful new image of Himself in us, unblemished and wrinkle-free.

MORNING
Wonderful Things

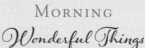

Everything God made is waiting with excitement
for God to show his children's glory completely.
ROMANS 8:19 NCV

Some days it's hard to feel very optimistic. We listen to the evening news and hear story after story about natural disasters and human greed. God doesn't want us to be ostriches, hiding our heads in the sand, refusing to acknowledge what's going on in the world. But He also wants us to believe that the future is full of wonderful things He has planned. The whole world is holding its breath, waiting for God's wonderful grace to reveal itself.

EVENING
Love Says No

"Anyone who loves their father or mother more than me is not worthy of me;
anyone who loves their son or daughter more than me is not worthy of me."
MATTHEW 10:37 NIV

Sometimes love has to be tough. It has to say no. It has to set limits. If you've been the parent of a teen, you know what it feels like to implement tough love. It's uncomfortable at times and can be a little tricky. You want that other person to know you love him or her, but you have to stick to your guns. God designed love to be both sweet and tough.

MORNING

Finishing with Joy

*But none of these things move me, neither count I my life
dear unto myself, so that I might finish my course with joy.*
ACTS 20:24 KJV

The Christian life is a journey, isn't it? We move from point A to
point B, and then on from there all the while growing in our faith.
Instead of focusing on the ups and downs of the journey, we should
be looking ahead, to the finish line. We want to be people who finish
well. Today, set your sights on that unseen line that lies ahead.
What joy will come when you cross it!

EVENING

This Is What Love Is. . .

*This is how we know what love is: Jesus Christ laid down his life for us.
And we ought to lay down our lives for our brothers.*
1 JOHN 3:16 NIV

Do you want to know what love is? It's the ability to sacrifice—to lay
down personal wants and wishes—for others. Jesus gave us the ultimate
example of sacrificial love when He walked up Calvary's hill and took
our place on the cross. When we let go of selfishness and pride and put
others first, we're following His lead. What an awesome display of love!

Morning
Holding Hands

When I am afraid, I will put my trust in You.
PSALM 56:3 NASB

While I cowered in a bathroom stall before my first speaking event,
my queasy stomach rolled and sweat beaded on my forehead. I prayed
for a way to escape. Into my head popped a childhood memory verse:
"When I am afraid, I will put my trust in You." My pounding heart
calmed. I repeated the scripture aloud and felt my nausea subside
and panic diminish. Peace flooded my soul. When we're afraid,
Papa God is right beside us holding our hand.

Evening
New Strength

"In quietness and confidence is your strength."
ISAIAH 30:15 NLT

The weaker we feel, the more we fret. The more we fret, the weaker
we feel. It's a vicious circle. Stop the circle! Find a quiet place,
if only for a few moments, to draw close to God. Grace will come
to you through the quiet, and you will discover new strength.

MORNING
The Details

She is clothed with strength and dignity,
and she laughs without fear of the future.
PROVERBS 31:25 NLT

God wants to clothe us with His strength, His dignity. He wants us to be whole and competent, full of His grace. When we are, we can look at the future and laugh, knowing that God will take care of the details as we trust Him to be the foundation of our lives.

EVENING
Wings

This means that anyone who belongs to Christ has become a new person.
The old life is gone; a new life has begun!
2 CORINTHIANS 5:17 NLT

Have you ever seen a butterfly crawling on her belly with caterpillars? Or trying desperately to hang on to her cocoon as she takes to the skies? Of course not—she spreads her wings and flies far away from her old life, discovering new and wonderful things she never knew existed. New life in Christ is full of discoveries and wonders, but you can't get there if you're still clutching the old life. It's time to let go, sister.

MORNING
The Joy of His Heart

For he shall not much remember the days of his life;
because God answereth him in the joy of his heart.

ECCLESIASTES 5:20 KJV

Sometimes we go through things that we wish we could forget. Hard things. Hurtful things. But God, in His remarkable way, eases the pain of our bumps in the road and before long, we can barely remember them. Joy rises up in place of pain, and we move forward, content in the fact that tomorrow will be better than yesterday. Don't focus on yesterday. Live for today and look forward to tomorrow.

EVENING
The Receiving End

And now, O Israel, what does the LORD your God ask of you
but to fear the LORD your God, to walk in obedience to him, to love him,
to serve the LORD your God with all your heart and with all your soul.

DEUTERONOMY 10:12 NIV

If you've hurt others, then perhaps you know what it feels like to be on the receiving end of some tough love. There are consequences to doing the wrong thing, and they often involve years of proving that you're trustworthy after letting someone down. Forgiveness and rebuilding trust take time. Receiving tough love is uncomfortable, but don't fight it. Let love win the battle. Relationships will be restored and hearts will be mended.

MORNING
Simply Happy

Are any of you happy?
You should sing praises.
JAMES 5:13 NLT

Some days are simply happy days. The sun shines, people make us laugh,
and life seems good. A day like that is a special grace. Thank God for it.
As you hum through your day, don't forget to sing His praises.

EVENING
A Crop of Love

"I said, 'Plant the good seeds of righteousness,
and you will harvest a crop of love.'"
HOSEA 10:12 NLT

Imagine yourself as a farmer out in the field planting good seeds.
What sort of crop do you think you will yield? An awesome one,
no doubt! Harvesting love is much like that. When we start with the
right attitude and a heart toward God and others, love always follows.
We need to start with softened hearts, though, so spend some time
today asking the Lord to break up the hard places.

MORNING
Excel in Giving

*But since you excel in everything—in faith, in speech,
in knowledge, in complete earnestness and in the love we have kindled in you—
see that you also excel in this grace of giving.*
2 CORINTHIANS 8:7 NIV

We want to excel at everything we do, and that takes effort on our part.
So we work to have excellent parenting skills. An excellent work ethic.
Excellent financial prowess. But what about giving? If we love God
and others, we should strive to become excellent givers. Want to excel
today? Consider giving of yourself to others.

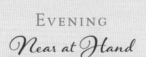

EVENING
Near at Hand

*Quiet down before GOD,
be prayerful before him.*
PSALM 37:7 MSG

It's not easy to be quiet. Our world is loud, and the noise seeps
into our hearts and minds. We feel restless and jumpy, on edge.
God seems far away. But God is always near at hand, no matter
how we feel. When we quiet our hearts, we will find Him there,
patiently waiting, ready to show us His grace.

MORNING
Righteousness, Peace, and Joy

For the kingdom of God is not meat and drink;
but righteousness, and peace, and joy in the Holy Ghost.
ROMANS 14:17 KJV

Sometimes life can be drudgery. We wake up in the morning.
Get dressed. Go to work (or stay home to care for our children).
We drag home in the evening, spend a little time with our loved ones,
then drop into bed, exhausted. Oh, there's so much more to life!
The Lord wants to remind you that He has given you righteousness,
peace, and joy. . .for every day of your life! So, celebrate!

EVENING
Look to the Sunrise

I rise before dawn and cry for help;
I have put my hope in your word.
PSALM 119:147 NIV

Could be stress or worry or berserk hormones. Whatever the cause,
many women find themselves staring at their dark bedroom ceilings
in the wee morning hours. We try counting sheep, but they morph
into naughty little children, and we exhaust ourselves chasing them
through fitful dreams. We're tormented by the *what ifs*, guilted by
the *should haves*, and jolted wider awake by the *don't forget tos*.
But a new day is dawning, and help is but a prayer away.

MORNING
Light My Fire

If God is for us, who can be against us?
ROMANS 8:31 NIV

Some days it feels as if the entire world is conspiring to make us as miserable as possible. Your spouse is crabby, the kids forget to mention the four dozen cupcakes they volunteered you for *today*, traffic jams, your boss is on the rampage, your coworkers are in nasty moods, you forgot to defrost dinner, the car overheats again. But our God is King of the Universe, and He's on our side. Girl, if that doesn't light your fire, the wood's wet.

EVENING
Love Is Patient

Love is patient, love is kind. It does not envy, it does not boast,
it is not proud. It does not dishonor others, it is not self-seeking,
it is not easily angered, it keeps no record of wrongs.
1 CORINTHIANS 13:4–5 NIV

Oh, how impatient we are! We want what we want—and we want it now! No waiting. But love isn't impatient. It doesn't demand immediate service. Instead, love waits patiently on the sidelines. The next time you feel yourself losing your patience, take a deep breath. Remind yourself: love holds on for the ride.

MORNING
Good for You!

A happy heart is like good medicine,
but a broken spirit drains your strength.
PROVERBS 17:22 NCV

God longs to make you happy. He knows that happiness is good for you. Mentally and physically, you function better when you are happy. Discouragement and sadness sap your strength. It's like trying to work while carrying a heavy load on your back: it slows you down and makes everything harder. Let God heal the breaks in your spirit. His grace can make you strong and happy.

EVENING
Let Love Flow!

"Just as the Father has loved Me,
I have also loved you; abide in My love."
JOHN 15:9 NASB

We love as we are loved. Think about that statement for a minute. We tend to share love to the same degree that we receive it. God pours out his love to us 24/7. His fountain of grace, love, and mercy flows freely. And as long as we continue to drink from that fountain, we will become a wellspring of life for others. Abide in Him. Let love flow!

MORNING

Everyday Joy

For in him we live, and move, and have our being.
ACTS 17:28 KJV

Every breath we breathe comes from God. Every step we take is a gift from our Creator. We can do nothing apart from Him. In the same sense, every joy, every sorrow. . .God goes through each one with us. His heart is for us. We can experience joy in our everyday lives, even when things aren't going our way. We simply have to remember that He is in control. We have our being. . .in Him!

EVENING

All Equal—By Grace

Live in peace with each other. Do not be proud, but make friends with those who seem unimportant. Do not think how smart you are.
ROMANS 12:16 NCV

Sometimes other people just seem so stupid! We pride ourselves that *we* would never act like that, dress like that, talk like that. But God wants us to let go of our pride. He wants us to remember that in His eyes we are all equal, all loved, all saved only by grace.

MORNING
Acing the Test

*Always be ready to give an answer
when someone asks you about your hope.*
1 PETER 3:15 CEV

Remember algebra tests in high school? Instant sweat and heart palpitations. You dreaded going into them unprepared; you wanted to have answers ready so you wouldn't be left with saliva drooling from your gaping mouth when questioned. The Bible says we should be prepared when someone asks about the hope within us—the hope they couldn't help but notice radiating from our souls. The answer scores an A+ for all eternity: Jesus!

EVENING
Desert Oasis

*Find rest in God;
my hope comes from him.*
PSALM 62:5 NIV

Rest. Far too elusive in our world of bustling busyness. Overwhelming responsibilities run us ragged. We find ourselves not just physically frazzled, but bankrupt of spirit. Exhaustion steals our joy. Like an oasis in the desert, our Father offers rest for our weary souls and restores our hope.

MORNING
Rescued!

The LORD wants to show his mercy to you. He wants to rise and comfort you.
The LORD is a fair God, and everyone who waits for his help will be happy.
ISAIAH 30:18 NCV

God doesn't want you to feel lonely and unhappy. He waits to bring
you close to Him, to comfort you, to forgive you. Wait for Him to rescue
you from life's unhappiness. His grace will never let you down.
Keep your eyes fixed on Him, and you will find happiness again.

EVENING
Patience and Understanding

Whoever is patient has great understanding,
but one who is quick-tempered displays folly.
PROVERBS 14:29 NIV

Ever wonder why some people are more understanding than others?
They're not quick-tempered. They take the time to think things
through. That's how love is. It doesn't knee-jerk. Doesn't react quickly.
Love responds with understanding and thoughtfulness, not foolish
words or a sharp retort. Take a deep breath, my friend!
Let love and patience rule the day!

MORNING
A Life of Joy

*You have greatly encouraged me and
made me happy despite all our troubles.*
2 CORINTHIANS 7:4 NLT

Want to know the perfect recipe for happiness? Spend your
days focused on making others happy. If you shift your focus from
yourself to others, you accomplish two things: you put others first,
and you're always looking for ways to make others smile. There's
something about spreading joy that satisfies the soul.

EVENING
A Necklace of Love

*Let love and faithfulness never leave you; bind them around your neck,
write them on the tablet of your heart. Then you will win
favor and a good name in the sight of God and man.*
PROVERBS 3:3–4 NIV

Have you ever had a really great necklace? Perhaps a relative or close
friend has passed one down to you. In some ways, love is like an
exquisite necklace, one you deliberately choose to wear. Each bead or
stone represents one person you've loved or someone you've forgiven.
It encircles you, reminding you of God's endless love. And it hangs near
your heart, a constant reminder that He is only a heartbeat away.

MORNING
Smiling in the Darkness

The hopes of the godless evaporate.
JOB 8:13 NLT

Hope isn't just an emotion; it's a perspective, a discipline, a way of life.
It's a journey of choice. We must learn to override those messages
of discouragement, despair, and fear that assault us in times of
trouble and press toward the light. Hope is smiling in the darkness.
It's confidence that faith in God's sovereignty amounts to
something. . .something life-changing, life-saving, and eternal.

EVENING
Because of Christ

*All this comes from the God who settled the relationship between us and him,
and then called us to settle our relationships with each other.*
2 CORINTHIANS 5:18 MSG

God created a bridge to span the distance between ourselves and Him.
That bridge is Christ, the best and fullest expression of divine grace.
Because of Christ, we are in a relationship with the Creator of the entire
world. And because of Christ, we are called to build bridges of our own,
to span the distance between ourselves and others.

MORNING
For Eternity

My health may fail, and my spirit may grow weak,
but God remains the strength of my heart; he is mine forever.
PSALM 73:26 NLT

Sooner or later, our bodies let us down. Even the healthiest of us will one day have to face old age. When our bodies' strength fails us, we may feel discouraged and depressed. But even then we can find joy and strength in our God. When our hearts belong to the Creator of the universe, we realize we are far more than our bodies. Because of God's unfailing grace, we will be truly healthy for all eternity.

EVENING
Chill

I lie awake thinking of you, meditating on you through the night.
Because you are my helper, I sing for joy in the shadow of your wings.
PSALM 63:6–7 NLT

Are you a worrier? Do you frequently find yourself working up a sweat building molehills into mountains during the midnight hours? This passage suggests an alternative for that nasty and unproductive habit. Instead of worrying, try meditating on the loving-kindness of God; allow the joy of being loved and protected to relax your tense muscles and ease you into peaceful rest.

MORNING
The Ways of Life

" 'You have made known to me the paths of life;
you will fill me with joy in your presence.' "
ACTS 2:28 NIV

God gives us everything we need to make it through life.
He teaches us His ways. Fills us with His joy. Gives us the pleasure
of meeting with Him for times of intimate worship. What an
awesome teacher and friend. He takes us by the hand and gently
leads us. . .from experience to experience. . .joy to joy.

EVENING
Joyful in Hope

Be joyful in hope, patient in affliction,
faithful in prayer.
ROMANS 12:12 NIV

Hope is a precious commodity, isn't it? When we're hopeful,
we can endure almost anything. It gives us the ability to patiently
endure even the toughest of challenges. And hope is also a wonderful
companion to love. When you love people, you find yourself treating
them with more patience. You're hopeful that the relationships God has
blessed you with are going to grow stronger and stronger as time goes by.

MORNING
Let Me Be

*"Martha…you are worried and upset about many things,
but few things are needed—or indeed only one.
Mary has chosen what is better."*
LUKE 10:41–42 NIV

Martha zipped around cleaning, cooking, and organizing. Meanwhile,
Mary sat at Jesus' feet. Many of us think like Martha. Will food
magically appear on the table? Will the house clean itself? We're slaves
to endless to-do lists. Our need to *do* overwhelms our desire to *be*.
Constipated calendars attest that we are human *doings* instead of
human *beings*. But Jesus taught that Mary chose best—simply to *be*.
Lord, help this *doer* learn to *be*.

EVENING
A Sweet-Smelling Offering

*Live a life of love just as Christ loved us and gave himself
for us as a sweet-smelling offering and sacrifice to God.*
EPHESIANS 5:2 NCV

What does it mean to live a life of love? For some it comes naturally.
Others have to work at it! Living a life of love means that you
pour yourself out like perfume as a fragrant offering—both to God
and to those around you. Your words taste and smell sweet. So do
your actions. You leave behind a pleasant aroma, and people
long to be around you. Mmm! Smell that love?

MORNING
Choosing Cheerful

A cheerful disposition is good for your health;
gloom and doom leave you bone-tired.
PROVERBS 17:22 MSG

Have you ever heard the saying "You may not be able to keep birds from perching on your head, but you can keep them from building nests in your hair"? It means we can't always control our emotions, but we *can* chose which ones we want to hold on to and dwell on. Choosing to be cheerful instead of gloomy is far healthier for our minds, bodies, and spirits. Being depressed is exhausting!

EVENING
Simply Love

But I am giving you a new command.
You must love each other, just as I have loved you.
JOHN 13:34 CEV

Christ doesn't ask us to point out others' faults. He doesn't require that we be the morality squad, focusing on all that is sinful in the world around us. Instead, He wants us to simply love, just as He loves us. When we do, the world will see God's grace shining in our lives.

MORNING
Christ Lives in Me

I am crucified with Christ: nevertheless I live;
yet not I, but Christ liveth in me.
GALATIANS 2:20 KJV

When you gave your heart to Christ, the old you the person you used
to be died. She's no longer alive. In a symbolic sense, you rose up out
of that experience with God as a new creature never again the same.
So, the life you now live isn't really your own. It's His!
And He lives in you. What a joyful exchange!

EVENING
Showers of Blessing

Do the skies themselves send down showers? No, it is you, LORD our God.
Therefore our hope is in you, for you are the one who does all this.
JEREMIAH 14:22 NIV

Have you ever stood in your parched garden, praying for rain?
The plants you've nurtured from seeds are wilting, flower petals litter
the ground, fruit withers on the vine. Then thunder clouds roll and the
skies burst forth with reinvigorating rain. There will be dry times, too,
in our spiritual gardens, when drought threatens to shrivel our faith.
But our hope is in the Lord our God, who sends showers to revive us.
Deluge us today, Lord.

Morning
Superglue Faith

In Him, you also, after listening to the message of truth,
the gospel of your salvation—having also believed,
you were sealed in Him with the Holy Spirit of promise.
EPHESIANS 1:13 NASB

Remember the old commercial that depicted a construction
worker dangling in midair, the top of his helmet bonded by
superglue to a horizontal beam? Faith is like superglue.
We cling to our God, our foundation, our beam. As believers,
we are sealed in Christ and the bond cannot be undone.
Through prayer in times of despair, our faith is strengthened
and becomes waterproof, pressure resistant, and unbreakable.

Evening
Built Up by Love

Love and faithfulness keep a king safe;
through love his throne is made secure.
PROVERBS 20:28 NIV

Did you know it takes a thousand "'Atta boys!" to overcome one
critical word? It's human nature to hang on to the negative words.
Criticism rings loud and clear in our ears, but not praise. That's why
it's so important to build others up with your love. Speak positive,
affirming words. Encourage. Uplift. Make the other person feel safe
and secure around you. Love doesn't tear down. It builds up.

MORNING
Whole and Healthy

When Jesus heard this, he told them, "Healthy people don't need a doctor—sick people do. I have come to call not those who think they are righteous, but those who know they are sinners."
MARK 2:17 NLT

With Jesus, we never need to pretend to be something we aren't. We don't need to impress Him with our spiritual maturity and mental acuity. Instead, we can come to Him honestly, with all our neediness, admitting just how weak we are. When we do, we let down the barriers that keep Him out of our hearts. We allow His grace to make us whole and healthy.

EVENING
Slow to Anger

The LORD is compassionate and gracious, slow to anger, abounding in love. He will not always accuse, nor will he harbor his anger forever; he does not treat us as our sins deserve or repay us according to our iniquities.
PSALM 103:8–10 NIV

One way to know you're "abounding" in God's love is to live a life that reflects His character. When you're slow to anger and refuse to knee-jerk when provoked, you're demonstrating His love. God doesn't treat us as we deserve (thank goodness!), and He expects that we will offer that same generosity to others, even when they wrong us. Don't repay evil for evil. Put the brakes on that anger!

MORNING
Blessings on the Merciful

"Blessed are the merciful, for they shall obtain mercy."
MATTHEW 5:7 NKJV

In some ways, mercy is like forgiveness. God offers it to the same extent we're willing to give it to others. The more merciful we are to those who wrong us, the more merciful God is to us. And blessings flow out of relationships that extend mercy. Want to experience true joy today? Give. . .and receive. . .mercy.

EVENING
Only by Grace

Accept one another, then, just as Christ accepted you,
in order to bring praise to God.
ROMANS 15:7 NIV

It's easy to pick out others' faults. Sometimes you may even feel justified in doing so, as though God will approve of your righteousness as you point out others' sinfulness. Don't forget that Christ accepted you, with all your brokenness and faults. Only by grace were you made whole. Share that grace—that acceptance and unconditional love— with the people around you.

MORNING

Small but Mighty

He has…exalted the humble.
LUKE 1:52 NLT

God delights in making small things great. He's in the business of taking scrap-heap people and turning them into treasures: Noah (the laughing stock of his city), Moses (stuttering shepherd turned national leader), David (smallest among the big and powerful), Sarah (old and childless), Mary (poor teenager), Rahab (harlot turned faith-filled ancestor of Jesus). So you and I can rejoice with hope! Let us glory in our smallness!

EVENING

Snippets of Hope

I also pray that you will understand the incredible greatness of God's power for us who believe him. This is the same mighty power that raised Christ from the dead and seated him in the place of honor at God's right hand in the heavenly realms.
EPHESIANS 1:19–20 NLT

Daydreams are snippets of hope for our souls. Yearnings for something better, something more exciting, something that lifts our spirits. Some dreams are mere fancy, but others are meant to last a lifetime because God embedded them in our hearts. It's when we lose sight of those dreams that hope dies. But God offers us access to His almighty power—the very same greatness that brought His Son back from the dead. What greater hope is there?

MORNING
Free!

For the Lord is the Spirit, and wherever the
Spirit of the Lord is, there is freedom.
2 CORINTHIANS 3:17 NLT

How do you know when the Holy Spirit is present in your life?
You should be able to tell by the sense of freedom you feel.
If you feel oppressed, obsessed, or depressed, something in your
life is out of kilter. Seek out God's Spirit. He wants you to be free.

EVENING
Only What Is Helpful

Do not let any unwholesome talk come out of your mouths,
but only what is helpful for building others up according
to their needs, that it may benefit those who listen.
EPHESIANS 4:29 NIV

Oh, how we love to talk about others. Usually we don't set out to gossip
or cause pain, but often that's how things end up. We get carried away.
We share our "concerns" with others. God longs for us to guard what we
say, dwelling only on what is helpful. That's how love operates. It compels
us to build others up, not cut them down. May every word be beneficial.

MORNING
Mercy Multiplied

Mercy unto you, and peace, and love, be multiplied.
JUDE 2 KJV

Have you ever done the math on God's mercy? If so, you've probably figured out that it just keeps multiplying itself out, over and over again. We mess up; He extends mercy. We mess up again; He pours out mercy once again. In the same way, peace, love, and joy are multiplied back to us. Praise the Lord! God's mathematics work in our favor.

EVENING
The Love Proof

*Dear children, let us not love with words
or speech but with actions and in truth.*
1 JOHN 3:18 NIV

It's one thing to tell people that you love them; it's another to live out that love with your actions. Sure, we say "I love you" all the time, but do we always follow those words up with the proof? Slipping up is easy, especially with people who are difficult to love. But God is always more interested in our actions than our words. He desires for us to love in word—and in deed.

MORNING
Keep Breathing, Sister!

As long as we are alive, we still have hope,
just as a live dog is better off than a dead lion.
ECCLESIASTES 9:4 CEV

Isn't this a tremendous scripture? At first glance, the ending elicits a chuckle. But consider the truth it contains: Regardless of how powerful, regal, or intimidating a lion is, when he's dead, he's *dead*. But the living—you and I—still have hope. Limitless possibilities! Hope for today and for the future. Although we may be as lowly dogs, fresh, juicy bones abound. As long as we're breathing, it's not too late!

EVENING
Move On

Anyone who belongs to Christ has become a new person.
The old life is gone; a new life has begun!
2 CORINTHIANS 5:17 NLT

You are a brand-new person in Jesus! Don't worry about what came before. Don't linger over your guilt and regret. Move on. Step out into the new, grace-filled life Christ has given you.

MORNING
Breathing

In certain ways we are weak, but the Spirit is here to help us.
For example, when we don't know what to pray for,
the Spirit prays for us in ways that cannot be put into words.
ROMANS 8:26 CEV

The Holy Spirit is the wind that blows through our world, breathing grace and life into everything that exists. He will breathe through you as well as you open yourself to Him. We need not worry about our own weakness or mistakes, for the Spirit will make up for them. His creative power will pray through us, work through us, and love through us.

EVENING
True Success

"For I know the plans I have for you," declares the LORD, "plans to prosper you and not to harm you, plans to give you hope and a future."
JEREMIAH 29:11 NIV

God doesn't call us to be successful; He calls us to trust Him. We may never be successful in the world's eyes, but trust in our Father's omnipotence ensures our future and our hope. And that's true success.

MORNING
Joy on That Glorious Day

Yea, all kings shall fall down before him:
all nations shall serve him.
PSALM 72:11 KJV

There's coming a day when every knee will bow and every tongue confess that Jesus Christ is Lord. Does it seem impossible right now, in light of current world events? If only we could see things the way God does! He knows that the kings of the nations will one day fall down before Him. Oh, what a glorious and joyful day that will be!

EVENING
Spur One Another On

And let us consider how we may spur one
another on toward love and good deeds.
HEBREWS 10:24 NIV

Do you have a friend who needs your encouragement?
One who needs a real boost? Ask yourself, "How can I spur her on?"
"What can I say that will make a difference?" Can you write her
a note of encouragement? Speak words of faith regarding her situation?
Love spurs us on, and words of kindness from a friend do the same.
Take time to build up your friend in love.

MORNING
It's a Mystery

This is the day which the LORD has made;
Let us rejoice and be glad in it.
PSALM 118:24 NASB

Let's face it, girls, some mornings our rejoicing lasts only until the toothpaste drips onto our new shirt or the toast sets off the fire alarm. But the mystery of Jesus-joy is that it's not dependent on rosy circumstances. If we, after cleaning the shirt and scraping the toast, intentionally give our day to the Lord, He *will* infuse it with His joy. Things look much better through Jesus-joy contact lenses!

EVENING
Nothing. . .or Everything?

If I speak in the tongues of men or of angels, but do not have love,
I am only a resounding gong or a clanging cymbal. If I have the gift of
prophecy and can fathom all mysteries and all knowledge, and if I have
a faith that can move mountains, but do not have love, I am nothing.
1 CORINTHIANS 13:1–2 NIV

It's one thing to claim to know God and to be called to a life of service to Him. It's another thing to back it up by loving the people He's placed in your life. You don't want to be a clanging gong (someone who talks the talk but doesn't walk the walk). Instead, be known as one who backs up her words with genuine love and compassion for others.

MORNING
His Instrument

"The Spirit of the Lord is on me, because he has anointed me to proclaim good news to the poor. He has sent me to proclaim freedom for the prisoners and recovery of sight for the blind, to set the oppressed free."
LUKE 4:18 NIV

Just as the Holy Spirit wants you to be free, He also wants to use you as His instrument to breathe freedom and hope into the world. Be His instrument today. Tell people the truly good news that God loves them. Do whatever you can to spread freedom and vision and hope. Be a vehicle of the Spirit's grace.

EVENING
Fresh Hearts

"I will give you a new heart and put a new spirit within you."
EZEKIEL 36:26 NKJV

Life is full of irritations and hassles. Bills to pay, chores to run, arguments to settle, and endless responsibilities all stress our hearts until we feel old and worn. But God renews us. Day after day, over and over, His grace comes to us, making our hearts fresh and green and growing.

MORNING
Joy in the Cities

And there was great joy in that city.
ACTS 8:8 KJV

Can you imagine the church of Jesus Christ alive and vibrant
in *every* city around the world? Alive in Moscow. Alive in Paris.
Alive in Havana. Alive. . .in your hometown. Oh, the celebration
that would ensue if cities around the world were eternally changed.
Today, choose a particular city and commit to pray for that place. . .
that all might come to know Him!

EVENING
Accolades

*Your Father, who sees what is
done in secret, will reward you.*
MATTHEW 6:4 NIV

The countless things we women do for our families are often not noticed
or appreciated. What a comfort to know that our Father sees *everything*,
no matter how small. Our reward may not be the Woman of the Year
award, or even hugs and kisses. It may not be here on earth at all. I'm
hoping it'll be a maid and cook for all eternity. But whatever it is,
we'll be *thrilled* because our Father is pleased with us.

MORNING

Top Off My Tank

"My grace is sufficient for you,
for my power is made perfect in weakness."
2 CORINTHIANS 12:9 NIV

There is no weaker vessel than a bedraggled mother at 6 a.m., staring into a bathroom mirror after another rough night. She's trying to decide if the dark smudges beneath her eyes are yesterday's grape jelly when she suddenly realizes she's brushing her hair with her toothbrush. Yep, we are a sisterhood of slightly sagging spiritual warriors, but we can depend on God to power our weak vessels. And He is able.

EVENING

A Satisfied Soul

Because your love is better than life, my lips will glorify you. I will praise
you as long as I live, and in your name I will lift up my hands. I will be fully
satisfied as with the richest of foods; with singing lips my mouth will praise you.
PSALM 63:3–5 NIV

Ah, satisfaction! Such a comforting feeling. Did you know that God wants us to be satisfied with His love? Our souls can be satisfied in Him. So what does it mean to be satisfied? It means we're okay with His plan, not ours. We trust in His love for us. He has our best interest at heart. Today allow the Lord's overwhelming love to satisfy your heart, your mind, and your soul.

MORNING

Spirit Oxygen

Tell me this one thing: How did you receive the Holy Spirit?
Did you receive the Spirit by following the law? No, you received
the Spirit because you heard the Good News and believed it.

GALATIANS 3:2 NCV

As we share the good news of Christ, we need to take care that we are not preaching the law rather than the love of Christ. The Spirit did not come into your heart through legalism and laws—and He won't reach others through you if that is your focus. Breathe deeply of grace, and let it spread from you to a world that is desperate for the oxygen of the Spirit.

EVENING

Genuine Love

You must teach people to have genuine love,
as well as a good conscience and true faith.

1 TIMOTHY 1:5 CEV

Isn't it interesting to read that we have to "teach" people to have genuine love? You would think it would come naturally! But genuine love is tougher than it's advertised to be. Real love is, after all, sacrificial. We enjoy a kiss on the cheek or a hurried "I love you" as we're hanging up the phone. But sacrifice? That's not as easy, is it? Allow genuine love to lead the way today!

MORNING
Praise Him, All You Nations!

All of you nations, come praise the LORD!
Let everyone praise him.
PSALM 117:1 CEV

Can you imagine the sound of millions of people, singing praises
to the Lord in thousands of different languages simultaneously?
On any given day, God hears people all over the world lift up their
praises to Him in their native tongues. Oh, what a joyful sound that
must be to our heavenly Father. Today, as you lift your voice, think of
the millions of others who join you. Praise Him! Oh, praise Him!

EVENING
From the Inside Out

Take on an entirely new way of life—a God-fashioned life,
a life renewed from the inside and working itself into your
conduct as God accurately reproduces his character in you.
EPHESIANS 4:24 MSG

At the end of a long week, we sometimes feel tired and drained,
as though all our creativity and energy have been robbed from us.
We need to use feelings like that as wake-up calls, reminders that
we need to open ourselves anew to God's Spirit so that He can
renew us from the inside out. Grace has the power to change our
hearts and minds, filling us with new energy to follow Jesus.

MORNING

Heavyweight

*This hope is like a firm and
steady anchor for our souls.*
HEBREWS 6:19 CEV

Hope in Christ is an anchor for our souls. But if the anchor isn't sturdy—weighted by firm and steady faith—we may drift in strong currents of doubt, problems, and disillusionment. Weigh your anchor today.

EVENING

Easy as ABC

*God has done all this, so that we will look for him and
reach out and find him. He isn't far from any of us.*
ACTS 17:27 CEV

God is near. But we must reach out for Him. There's a line that we choose to cross, a specific action we take. We can't ooze into the kingdom of God; it's an intentional decision. It's simple, really—as simple as ABC. A is *Admitting* we're sinful and in need of a Savior. B is *Believing* that Jesus died for our sins and rose from the grave. C is *Committing* our lives to Him. Life everlasting is then ours.

MORNING

A Lovely Place

How lovely is your dwelling place, LORD Almighty!
PSALM 84:1 NIV

Imagine this: God considers your heart His home!
It's the place where He dwells. And as a result, your heart
is a lovely place, filled with the grace of the almighty God.

EVENING

Be Glad!

Satisfy us in the morning with your unfailing love,
that we may sing for joy and be glad all our days.
PSALM 90:14 NIV

Can you imagine waking up satisfied every morning? God's unfailing love can cause you to do that. You can wake up with a song on your lips and a happy heart. Why? Because His love sustains you through the night. It gets you through the dark places. The valleys. You awake to a new day, fresh with His love and His insight. Ah, morning! What a wonderful time to praise!

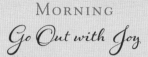

MORNING
Go Out with Joy

For ye shall go out with joy, and be led forth with peace:
the mountains and the hills shall break forth before you
into singing, and all the trees of the field shall clap their hands.
ISAIAH 55:12 KJV

God reveals Himself in a million different ways, but perhaps
the most breathtaking is through nature. The next time you're in
a mountainous spot, pause and listen. Can you hear the sound
of God's eternal song? Does joy radiate through your being?
Aren't you filled with wonder and with peace? The Lord has,
through the beauty of nature, given us a rare and glorious gift.

EVENING
His Profound Love

I pray that you, being rooted and established in love, may have power,
together with all the Lord's holy people, to grasp how wide and long
and high and deep is the love of Christ, and to know this love that surpasses
knowledge—that you may be filled to the measure of all the fullness of God.
EPHESIANS 3:17–19 NIV

Have you ever paused to contemplate God's unfathomable love for
us? If we could climb to the top of the highest mountain, we couldn't
outclimb His love. If we plummeted to the depths, His love would
meet us there. If our vision could expand to see beyond the stars,
we would find His love waiting there for us. There is truly nothing
to compare with the profound love of our Savior!

MORNING
A Special Place

*My people will live in peaceful places and
in safe homes and in calm places of rest.*
ISAIAH 32:18 NCV

Home is the place where you feel most comfortable—the place
where you can kick off your shoes, put on your bathrobe,
and relax. God has created this place for you, a place where
His grace can soothe your heart in a special way.

EVENING
Drawing Back the Curtains

*But whenever someone turns to the Lord, the veil is taken away. . . .
So all of us who have had that veil removed can see and reflect the
glory of the Lord. And the Lord—who is the Spirit—makes us more
and more like him as we are changed into his glorious image.*
2 CORINTHIANS 3:16, 18 NLT

Sometime we feel as though a thick dark curtain hangs between
us and God, hiding Him from our sight. But the Bible says that all
we have to do is turn our hearts to the Lord and the curtain will
be drawn back, letting God's glory and grace shine into our lives.
When that happens, we can soak up the light, allowing it to
renew our hearts and minds into the image of Christ.

MORNING
Unquenchable Love

Many waters cannot quench love; rivers cannot sweep it away. If one were to give all the wealth of his house for love, it would be utterly scorned.
SONG OF SONGS 8:7 NIV

Have you ever been so thirsty that a cup of water didn't satisfy you? If so, then you have some understanding of how love works. The more you have of it, the more you want. And God's love for us is so overpowering that nothing we do can wash it away. Talk about amazing love! Lift up your voice in praise for the love you've been shown.

EVENING
Bestseller

The mystery is that Christ lives in you,
and he is your hope of sharing in God's glory.
COLOSSIANS 1:27 CEV

Everybody loves a good mystery—as long as the plot twists a bit and the good guy wins in the end. The Christian life is a mystery. It's baffling that God could love us so deeply that He sent His only Son to suffer and die for us. And now the risen Christ lives in our hearts, bridging the gap between us and God forever. What an incredible page-turner!

MORNING
Sing, O Heavens!

Sing, O heavens; and be joyful, O earth; and break forth into singing,
O mountains: for the LORD hath comforted his people,
and will have mercy upon his afflicted.

ISAIAH 49:13 KJV

Imagine you're walking through a meadow on a dewy morning. The sweet smell of dawn lingers in the air. Suddenly, like a skilled orchestra, the heavens above begin to pour out an unexpected song of joy. You close your eyes, overwhelmed by the majesty of the moment. Scripture tells us the heavens and the earth are joyful. . .so tune in to their chorus today.

EVENING
Joyful Are Those

Praise the LORD! How joyful are those who fear the LORD and delight
in obeying his commands. Their children will be successful everywhere;
an entire generation of godly people will be blessed.

PSALM 112:1–2 NLT

When we're fully aware of God's love for us—and for our children—we can be more than satisfied. We can be joyful! Why? Because He has us covered. He sees our needs and meets them. He loves us with an everlasting love. And His blessings aren't just for us; they're for an entire generation of godly people! Talk about a reason to celebrate!

Morning
Brick by Brick

So then faith cometh by hearing,
and hearing by the word of God.
ROMANS 10:17 KJV

Words are powerful. They cut. They heal. They confirm. God uses His Word to help us, to mold us, to make us more like Him. Our faith is built from the bricks of God's Word. Brick by brick, we erect, strengthen, and fortify that faith. But only if we truly listen and *hear* the Word of God.

Evening
Hearts Filled with Love

And this hope will not lead to disappointment.
For we know how dearly God loves us, because he has
given us the Holy Spirit to fill our hearts with his love.
ROMANS 5:5 NLT

Have you ever doubted God's love for you? Wondered if He's still there, looking out for you? One way you can know for sure that God loves you is to recognize His gift of the Holy Spirit, who resides inside you. God sent the Spirit, our Comforter, so that we would know we're never alone. Talk about a precious reminder of God's love!

MORNING
Longing for Home

This is what the LORD says: "You will be in Babylon for seventy years. But then I will come and do for you all the good things I have promised, and I will bring you home again."
JEREMIAH 29:10 NLT

Sometimes in life we go through periods when we feel out of place, as though we just don't belong. Our hearts feel restless and lonely. We long to go home, but we don't know how. God uses those times to teach us special things we need to know. But He never leaves us in exile. His grace always brings us home.

EVENING
Quiet, Gentle Grace

"Let me teach you, because I am humble and gentle at heart, and you will find rest for your souls."
MATTHEW 11:29 NLT

Sometimes we keep trying to do things on our own, even though we don't know what we're doing and even though we're exhausted. And all the while, Jesus waits quietly, ready to show us the way. He will lead us with quiet, gentle grace, carrying our burdens for us. We don't have to try so hard. We can finally rest.

MORNING
Nature's Joys

The heavens declare the glory of God;
the skies proclaim the work of his hands.
PSALM 19:1 NIV

Oh, the wonder of God's creation! Who could paint the skies such a brilliant blue? And who could give such detail to such a tiny blade of grass? Only our creative Lord! Spend some time outdoors with Him today, soaking in the beauty of your surroundings. Allow the joy to permeate your soul, and give thanks to our awesome God, Creator of all.

EVENING
Beautify

For the LORD takes pleasure in His people;
He will beautify the afflicted ones with salvation.
PSALM 149:4 NASB

Our Lord takes pleasure in our company, despite our inabilities, unsightliness, or neediness. Hard to believe He actually *chooses* our company, but He does! And in spending time with us, He beautifies us with His lovely countenance.

MORNING

A Perfect Fit

The LORD is good to those whose hope is in him,
to the one who seeks him.

LAMENTATIONS 3:25 NIV

Seeking God is, for some, like a child groping in a dark room for the light switch. She knows it's there, she just can't seem to put her fingers on it. Some search for God all their lives, trying on various religions like pairs of shoes. This one pinches. That one chafes. But we must bypass religious fluff for the heart of the matter: Jesus. The only way to God is through faith in Christ (John 14:6). Suddenly, the shoe fits!

EVENING

With Long Life

"With a long life I will satisfy him
and let him see My salvation."

PSALM 91:16 NASB

Have you ever seen the look of contentment in the face of an older believer? Next time you're around someone in his golden years, take time to examine his expression. What you will find is contentment. Satisfaction. He's walked with God a long time and knows that the Lord won't leave or forsake him. He has seen God's salvation in this lifetime and looks forward to heaven, which is right around the bend.

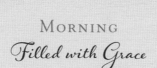

Morning
Filled with Grace

"There is plenty of room for you in my Father's home. If that weren't so, would I have told you that I'm on my way to get a room ready for you?"
John 14:2 msg

None of us knows exactly what lies on the other side of death's dark door. But we do know this: death will take us home. Jesus promised us that. He wouldn't have said it just to make us feel better; Jesus wasn't one for telling polite lies! So we can trust that right now He is getting our home in heaven ready for us, filling it with grace. When we enter the door, we will find it is exactly right for us, the place for which we have always longed.

Evening
She Who Loves Her Husband...

Older women must train the younger women to love their husbands and children.
Titus 2:4 nlt

In biblical times, young women often married older men, and not usually for love. They were betrothed based on selections made by the father. No wonder they would have to "train" to love their husbands! Love would grow over time after the couple took their vows. Things are different today, but we all still need time to mature in our love. Real love continues to grow over time.

MORNING
Second Chances

For his anger lasts only a moment, but his favor lasts a lifetime;
weeping may stay for the night, but rejoicing comes in the morning.
PSALM 30:5 NIV

Don't you love second chances? New beginnings? If only we could go
back and redo some of our past mistakes. . .what better choices we'd
make the second time around. Life in Jesus is all about the rebirth
experience—the opportunity to start over. Each day is a new day, in fact.
And praise God! The sorrows and trials of yesterday are behind us.
With each new morning, joy dawns!

EVENING
Take a Break

"Only in returning to me and
resting in me will you be saved."
ISAIAH 30:15 NLT

Some days you try everything you can think of to save yourself, but
no matter how hard you try, you fail again and again. You fall on your
face and embarrass yourself. You hurt the people around you. You make
mistakes, and nothing whatsoever seems to go right. When that happens,
it's time to take a break. You need to stop trying so hard. Throw yourself
in God's arms. Rest on His grace, knowing that He will save you.

MORNING
Legacy of Love

*After all, when the Lord Jesus appears, who else but you
will give us hope and joy and be like a glorious crown for us?*
1 THESSALONIANS 2:19 CEV

The most hope-inspiring legacy we can pass on to the next
generation is faith. What delight it is for us as women to plant
and nurture seeds of faith in our children, knowing that at
harvest they'll stand by our sides before the Lord Jesus! It's never
too late to till the fertile soil of their hearts by our example of
daily Bible reading, prayer, and dependence on our Savior.

EVENING
Survivor

*The terrible storm raged for many days, blotting out
the sun and the stars, until at last all hope was gone.*
ACTS 27:20 NLT

Following a lovely renewal of our wedding vows on our tenth
anniversary, my husband and I boarded a Caribbean cruise ship.
Tragically, Hurricane Gilbert obliterated our destination, Cancun,
before hurling our ship back and forth on twelve-foot waves for
four interminable days. I felt hopeless, sick as a pup, and at the mercy
of the storm. Life's like that, isn't it? Unexpected storms blow up,
blot out the light, and toss us about. But we are survivors!

MORNING
Unchanged

Why am I discouraged? Why is my heart so sad?
I will put my hope in God!
PSALM 42:5 NLT

Thousands of years ago, the psalmist who wrote these words expressed the same feelings we all have. Some days we just feel blue. The world looks dark, everything seems to be going wrong, and our hearts are sad. Those feelings are part of the human condition. Like the psalmist, we need to remind ourselves that God is unchanged by cloudy skies and gloomy hearts. His grace is always the same, as bright and hopeful as ever.

EVENING
Under the Shadow

How precious is your unfailing love, O God!
All humanity finds shelter in the shadow of your wings.
PSALM 36:7 NLT

People fail us. They say they're going to do something, and then they don't. They promise to stick with us, and then they leave. We even fail others, making promises we don't keep. But God isn't a failure, and neither is His love. We can trust in His unfailing love. In fact, we can live under its shadow all the days of our lives!

MORNING

Exceeding Great Joy

When they saw the star, they rejoiced with exceeding great joy.
MATTHEW 2:10 KJV

Can you imagine the wise men, gazing upon that star for the first time? Finally! The long-awaited day had come. What joy they must have felt in their hearts. Surely they could sense the beginning of a new era. The Gospel message is all about new beginnings. We rejoice every time we're given a chance to begin again. Praise God for the many times He's given you a fresh start.

EVENING

Sum It Up!

The commandments, "Do not commit adultery," "You shall not murder," "You shall not steal," "You shall not covet," and whatever other command there may be, are summed up in this one command: "Love your neighbor as yourself." Love does no harm to a neighbor. Therefore love is the fulfillment of the law.
ROMANS 13:9–10 NIV

"Love your neighbor as yourself." We've heard these familiar words all of our lives, but what do they mean? And, who is our neighbor? The guy in the house next door? The woman at the grocery store? Our neighbors are those people we see day in and day out. God desires that we love them in the very same way we love ourselves. Today ask the Lord to show you how to love your neighbors.

MORNING
I've Got a Name

"I have redeemed you; I have called
you by your name; you are Mine."
ISAIAH 43:1 NKJV

Parents have the indescribable privilege of bestowing a name on their newborn. The identity that little person will be known by for the rest of his or her life. In effect, we give them a part of us. They are an extension of ourselves—our flesh, our blood. Your heavenly Father has called you by name. He has given you part of Himself: Jesus. You are special to Him. You are His daughter. In this, find security. . .comfort. . .hope.

EVENING
Sleep in Peace

At day's end I'm ready for sound sleep,
For you, GOD, have put my life back together.
PSALM 4:8 MSG

At the end of the day, let everything—good and bad together—drop into God's hands. You can sleep in peace, knowing that meanwhile God will continue to work, healing all that is broken in your life. Relax in His grace.

MORNING
Amazing Expectations

Listen to my voice in the morning, LORD.
Each morning I bring my requests to you and wait expectantly.
PSALM 5:3 NLT

You need to get in the habit of hoping. Instead of getting up in the morning and sighing as you face another dreary day, practice saying hello to God as soon as you wake up. Listen for what He wants to say to your heart. Expect Him to do amazing things each day.

EVENING
Living Hope

Now faith is confidence in what we hope
for and assurance about what we do not see.
HEBREWS 11:1 NIV

This beloved scripture has long been the Christian's definition of faith. But if reworked a smidge, it's also the meaning of hope in Christ: hope is confidence in whom we have placed our faith and assurance of what we do not see. We don't see fragrance or love or blood flowing through our bodies, but we're certain of their existence. We can't see hope, but there's no doubt when it's alive within us. Praise God for living hope!

MORNING
On Wings of Joy

*"All the earlier troubles, chaos, and pain are things of the past,
to be forgotten. Look ahead with joy. Anticipate what I'm creating."*
ISAIAH 65:17–18 MSG

We don't always get it right, do we? Sometimes we make mistakes. But our mistakes spur us on to begin again. We want to get it right the next time. And praise God! He gives us chance after chance, opportunity after opportunity. Let the joys of your past successes merge with the "spurs" of your past failings so that you can set out on a road of new beginnings.

EVENING
Trust in His Love

*But I trust in your unfailing love;
my heart rejoices in your salvation.*
PSALM 13:5 NIV

Some of us have trust issues, don't we? We've been let down
so many times, we have trouble trusting anyone, even God.
Here's the good news: God is trustworthy! He won't let you down.
Won't leave you hanging. We can trust in His unfailing love,
and we can trust that He's going to do what He has promised.

MORNING
His Little Girls

Just as a father has compassion on his children,
so the LORD has compassion on those who fear Him.
PSALM 103:13 NASB

Plagued with horrible recurring nightmares during my childhood,
I remember the terror of waking up screaming, hair sweat-plastered to
my face. Then like a candle in the darkness, my father would appear at
my bedside, lie beside me, and gently rub my back until I fell asleep. Our
heavenly Father is like that—tender, caring, protective. And He, too,
responds when His little girls need comfort from His loving presence.

EVENING
Love for the Church

We know that we have passed out of death into life, because we
love the brothers. Whoever does not love abides in death.
1 JOHN 3:14 ESV

Our brothers and sisters in Christ should be like family members
to us. And like family members, they're not always easy to love!
But loving fellow church members is the best way to show
that we love God. If we love Him, we should love His kids.
This is how we know that we are alive in Christ.

MORNING
An Attitude

God proves to be good to the man who passionately waits,
to the woman who diligently seeks. It's a good thing
to quietly hope, quietly hope for help from God.
LAMENTATIONS 3:25 MSG

Hope is an attitude, not an emotion. It means putting our whole
hearts into relying on God. It means keeping our eyes focused on
Him no matter what, waiting for Him to reveal Himself in our lives.
God never disappoints those who passionately wait for His help,
who diligently seek His grace.

EVENING
Welcome Interruptions

So they left by boat for a quiet place,
where they could be alone.
MARK 6:32 NLT

Jesus and the disciples sought a quiet place, away from the crowds.
Like us, they needed alone time. But as so often happens, people
interrupt those moments of solitude. The crowd follows us, the phone
rings, someone comes to the door. When that happens, we must
ask Jesus for the grace to follow His example and let go of our quiet
moments alone, welcoming the interruption with patience and love.

MORNING
The New Man

*And have put on the new self, which is being
renewed in knowledge in the image of its Creator.*
COLOSSIANS 3:10 NIV

Are there people in your life you've given up on? Maybe someone
you've been praying for, for years? You're convinced he or she will
never come to the Lord? Today, ponder the new beginnings in your
own life. Hasn't God re-created you? Renewed you? Won't He do the
same for others? Feel the joy rise up as you ponder the possibilities?
Pray for that friend or loved one to "put on the new self."

EVENING
Band-Aids

*We have run to God for safety. Now his promises should greatly
encourage us to take hold of the hope that is right in front of us.*
HEBREWS 6:18 CEV

Have you ever lost your glasses or your keys and looked everywhere for
them, only to have someone point out that they're right in front of you?
God's hope is like that—right in front of us, but we don't always see
it. Our eyes are too busy searching for things we *think* will infuse hope:
financial security, makeovers, losing weight, marriage, a new baby.
But these are only Band-Aids. Our *true* hope is in Christ alone.

MORNING
His Heart's Delight

The LORD's delight is in those who fear him,
those who put their hope in his unfailing love.
PSALM 147:11 NLT

Do you remember how you felt when you witnessed a baby's first faltering steps? *Delight.* That's what it was. Just like when you heard her sing "Jesus Loves Me" in her squeaky, off-key voice, or she served you tea in tiny pink teacups. The Bible says the Lord delights in us, His children, the very same way. We warm His heart and bring a smile to His lips when we honor Him with our lives. He *delights* in us.

EVENING
Love as You Say You Love

Many claim to have unfailing love,
but a faithful person who can find?
PROVERBS 20:6 NIV

"I love yous" are a dime a dozen. We hear them on TV, read them in books, and see them in gossip magazines. Everyone is in love, though usually not for long. Though they say the words, many would-be lovers change their minds after a short time. If you're looking for a "forever" kind of love, look to God. He loves as He says He loves, and He can teach you to do the same!

MORNING
Grace of Hospitality

When God's people are in need, be ready to help them.
Always be eager to practice hospitality.
ROMANS 12:13 NLT

God opens Himself to you, offering you everything He has,
and He calls you to do the same for others. Just as He made you
welcome, make others welcome in your life. Don't reach out to
others grudgingly, with a sense of obligation. Instead, be eager
for opportunities to practice the grace of hospitality.

EVENING
Brothers and Sisters

Respect everyone, and love the family of believers.
Fear God, and respect the king.
1 PETER 2:17 NLT

Families have squabbles even under the best of circumstances.
The same holds true in the body of Christ. We're one big happy
family with God as our Father, but sometimes we disagree. We even
argue. Loving someone doesn't mean you'll always see eye to eye,
but it does mean you respect the other person and treat him or
her with dignity. Now, that's God's kind of love!

MORNING
Joyful Obedience

Now unto him that is able to keep you from falling, and to present you faultless before the presence of his glory with exceeding joy.
JUDE 24 KJV

Our obedience makes God happy and should make us happy, too. In fact, the more difficult it is to obey, the more joyful we should be. Why? Because a big situation calls for a big God. And our God is bigger than anything we could ask or think. He alone can prevent us from falling. So, if you're struggling in the area of obedience, surrender your will. Enter into joyful obedience.

EVENING
Mind, Body, Spirit...

I stretch myself out. I sleep.
Then I'm up again—rested, tall and steady.
PSALM 3:5 MSG

Rest is one of God's gifts to us, a gift we regularly need.
In sleep, we are renewed, mind, body, and spirit.
Don't turn away from this most natural and practical of gifts!

Morning
Rest Stop

So let's not allow ourselves to get fatigued doing good. At the right time we will harvest a good crop if we don't give up, or quit.
GALATIANS 6:9 MSG

As women, we're used to serving others. It's part of the feminine package. But sometimes we get burned out. Fatigued. Overburdened. Girls, God doesn't want us to be washed-out dishrags, to be so boggled that we try to pay for groceries with our Blockbuster card. It's up to us to recognize the symptoms and rest, regroup, reenergize. This is not indulgent; it's *necessary* to do our best in His name. So give yourself permission to rest. Today.

Evening
Prune Juice, Anyone?

Therefore, with minds that are alert and fully sober set your hope on the grace to be brought to you when Jesus Christ is revealed.
1 PETER 1:13 NIV

In the fruit bowl of the Spirit, self-control is the prune. It's hard to swallow but nonetheless essential to our faith—especially where hope is concerned. If self-control isn't exercised, we can find our spirits soaring up and down faster than the numbers on our bathroom scales. Like prunes, daily use of self-control regulates us and prepares us for action.

MORNING

Open Homes

Be quick to give a meal to the hungry, a bed to the homeless—cheerfully.
1 PETER 4:9 MSG

Because our homes are our private places, the places we retreat to when we're tired to find new strength, it's hard sometimes to open our homes to others. It's bad enough that we have to cope with others' needs all day long, we feel, without having to bring them home with us! But God calls us to offer our hospitality, and He will give us the grace to do it joyfully.

EVENING

Silenced by Love

In your unfailing love, silence my enemies;
destroy all my foes, for I am your servant.
PSALM 143:12 NIV

God's unfailing love is powerful. It can cause us to rise up and shout for joy, and it can silence our enemies in a second. When we follow after the Lord, His love comes with a "protective" feature: it stops our enemies in their tracks. Oh, it might not happen right away, but love eventually wins out!

Morning
Used for a Purpose

*Become the kind of container God can use to present
any and every kind of gift to his guests for their blessing.*
2 TIMOTHY 2:21 MSG

Want to reach the end of your life feeling completely fulfilled?
Want to know true joy? Then allow the Lord to use you. Does that
idea contradict what you've been taught in this "me first" society?
Being "used" by God is far different from being "used" by people.
Being usable is our goal, our ambition. Today, offer your gifts and
abilities to the Lord so that they can be used for His purpose.

Evening
Our Pursuit

*Whoever pursues righteousness and
love finds life, prosperity and honor.*
PROVERBS 21:21 NIV

Want to be respected in the workplace? Want to garner the right
attention from coworkers and the boss? Try righteousness and love.
Stand up for what's right. If you pursue righteousness (even when
others around you are succumbing to temptation), and if you genuinely
love your fellow workers, you will come out a winner in the end.
No, the road won't always be easy, but it will be worth it.

MORNING
Let the Sun Shine In

*Come to me, all you who are weary
and burdened, and I will give you rest.*
MATTHEW 11:28 NIV

Nothing chokes hope like weariness. Day in and day out drudgery produces weariness of body, heart, and soul. It feels like dark clouds have obscured the sun and cast us into perpetual shadow. But Jesus promised rest for our weary souls, respite from our burdens and healing for our wounds. . .*if* we come to Him. The sun isn't really gone, it's just hidden until the clouds roll away.

EVENING
Always Present

*LORD, you have been watching. Do not keep quiet.
Lord, do not leave me alone.*
PSALM 35:22 NCV

Have you ever seen a child suddenly look up from playing, realize she's all alone, and then run to get her mother's attention? Meanwhile, her mother was watching her all along. Sometimes solitude is a good thing—and other times, it's just plain lonely. When loneliness turns into isolation, remember that God's loving eyes are always on you. He will never leave you all alone, and His grace is always present.

MORNING
Everyone

If your enemy is hungry, feed him.
If he is thirsty, give him a drink.
PROVERBS 25:21 NCV

It's easy to have our friends over for dinner. Offering our hospitality to the people who give us pleasure is not much of a hardship. But hospitality gets harder when we offer it to the people who hurt our feelings, the people we really don't like very much. But God calls us to reach out in practical, tangible ways to *everyone*. Seek His grace to do this in some way every day.

EVENING
No Shame

No one who hopes in
you will ever be put to shame.
PSALM 25:3 NIV

Some of us have A- temperaments. We're not quite as flamboyant as type A personalities or as pensive as type B, but because of our tendency to rev our tongues into overdrive before getting our brains in gear, we spend a lot of time extracting foot from mouth. God implores us to control our tongues; the tiny sparks that inflame forests; the rudders that control enormous ships—our means of shame or glorifying His name!

MORNING
Give 'Em Something to Talk About

Everyone has heard about your obedience, so I rejoice because of you;
but I want you to be wise about what is good, and innocent about what is evil.
ROMANS 16:19 NIV

Ever been caught in a situation where people were talking about
you behind your back? Maybe folks you loved and trusted? How did
that make you feel? Well, how would you feel if you found out people
were talking about you. . .because of your obedience? Wow! That's a
different thing altogether. Let them talk! May our joyful obedience
to the Lord win us a spot in many cheerful conversations!

EVENING
Unshaken—and Unfailing

"Though the mountains be shaken and the hills be removed,
yet my unfailing love for you will not be shaken nor my covenant
of peace be removed," says the LORD, *who has compassion on you.*
ISAIAH 54:10 NIV

Life doesn't always go the way we hope it does. We face storms.
Challenges. We're wounded by people we love, and we feel like curling
up in a ball and forgetting about life. God's unfailing love woos us from
our place of pain and reminds us that the shaking won't last forever.
His covenant of peace lasts forever. We really can be unshaken,
as long as we abide in His unfailing love.

MORNING
No Wimps Here

For God has not given us a spirit of fear and timidity,
but of power, love, and self-discipline.
2 TIMOTHY 1:7 NLT

Do you suffer paralysis by analysis? Are you so afraid of trying something new that you put it off until you can think it through. . .and end up doing nothing at all? Too much introspection creates inertia, and we abhor the ineffective wimps we become. Sisters, God never intended for us to be wimps. His power and love are available to replace our fear and infuse us with courage. Shake off that paralysis and get moving!

EVENING
A Growing Love

Dear brothers and sisters, we can't help but thank God for you,
because your faith is flourishing and your love for one another is growing.
2 THESSALONIANS 1:3 NLT

Sometimes office relationships can wane over time. Maybe you start out as friends, but the stresses of the environment cause a deterioration in the friendship. If you want to maintain great interoffice friendships that grow even stronger with time, you have to keep brotherly love in the forefront. It won't always be easy, but it will be worth it.

MORNING
Thinking Habits

And now, dear brothers and sisters, one final thing. Fix your thoughts on what is true, and honorable, and right, and pure, and lovely, and admirable. Think about things that are excellent and worthy of praise.
PHILIPPIANS 4:8 NLT

Our brains are gifts from God, intended to serve us well, special gifts of grace we often take for granted. In return, we need to offer our minds back to God. Practice thinking positive thoughts. Focus on what is true rather than on lies; pay attention to beautiful things and stop staring at the ugly things in life. Discipline your minds to take on God's habits of thinking.

EVENING
The Right People

The LORD God said, "It isn't good for the man to live alone. I need to make a suitable partner for him."
GENESIS 2:18 CEV

God understands that human beings need each other. His love comes to us through others. That is the way He designed us, and we can trust His grace to bring the right people along when we need them, the people who will banish our loneliness and share our lives.

MORNING
Years of Pleasure

*If they obey and serve him, they shall spend their
days in prosperity, and their years in pleasures.*
JOB 36:11 KJV

If you knew that your disobedience was going to cost you dearly,
would you be more inclined to obey? If you knew that your
obedience would be rewarded, would that spur you on to do the
right thing? Scripture convinces us that our days can be spent in
prosperity and our years in pleasures if we will simply obey
and serve the Lord. Oh, the joy of obedience!

EVENING
True Colors

*May integrity and honesty protect me,
for I put my hope in you.*
PSALM 25:21 NLT

We sometimes hide little acts of dishonesty—taking the bank's
pen, pocketing that extra dollar from the clerk's mistake,
fudging tax figures. But our integrity is on display at all times to
the One who gave His life for us. When our true colors are
exposed in the Son-light, we want to shimmer, too.

MORNING
Battle Plan

I sought the LORD, and He answered me,
and delivered me from all my fears.
PSALM 34:4 NASB

There is nothing more wasteful than fear. Fear paralyzes, destroys potential, and shatters hope. It's like an enemy attacking from our blind side. But we don't have to allow fear to defeat us. It's a war that we can win! First comes earnest prayer, then comes change. God will deliver us from our fears if we seek Him and follow His battle plan.

EVENING
With All Your Heart

Jesus said to him, "'You shall love the LORD your God with all your heart, with all your soul, and with all your mind.' This is the first and great commandment. And the second is like it: 'You shall love your neighbor as yourself.' On these two commandments hang all the Law and the Prophets."
MATTHEW 22:37–40 NKJV

Jesus commands us to do two things: love God and love others. That seems so simple, yet it's so hard! If we truly loved God with all of our hearts—laying down our own wants, wishes and desires—it would revolutionize our lives! Here's the great part: it's possible to live like this! Love God. Love people. Watch as God transforms your world!

MORNING
All of You

*"'Love the Lord God with all your passion
and prayer and intelligence and energy.'"*
MARK 12:30 MSG

God wants all of you. He wants the "spiritual parts," but He
also wants your emotions, your physical energy, and your
brain's intelligence. Offer them all to God as expressions of
your love for Him. Let His grace use every part of you!

EVENING
Disciple the Nations

*Therefore go and make disciples of all nations, baptizing them
in the name of the Father and of the Son and of the Holy Spirit.*
MATTHEW 28:19 NIV

To truly disciple people, we have to love them. Otherwise, we won't go
the distance with them. It's a day-in, day-out process that can be grueling.
We're commanded by Jesus to go and make disciples of all nations—
not converts, disciples. Love compels us to go the distance by offering
financial support to missionaries or by making the commitment to go
ourselves. Today pray about the role you play in reaching the nations.

MORNING
Uprightness

"I know also, my God, that You test the heart and have pleasure in uprightness."
1 CHRONICLES 29:17 NKJV

Everyone wants to be happy, right? We know that our obedience to the Lord results in a life of great joy. But our obedience does something else, too. It brings pleasure to our heavenly Father. When we live uprightly, God is pleased. Today, instead of focusing on your own happiness, give some thought to putting a smile on *His* face.

EVENING
All Alone

"But when you pray, go away by yourself, shut the door behind you, and pray to your Father in private. Then your Father, who sees everything, will reward you."
MATTHEW 6:6 NLT

Prayer takes many shapes and forms. There's the corporate kind of prayer, in which we stand in a pew in a church, lifting our hearts to God as part of a congregation. There is also the far less elaborate kind of prayer that is said quickly and on the run; the whispered cry for help or song of praise in the midst of life's busyness. But we need to make at least some time in our lives for the prayer that comes out of solitude, when, in the privacy of some quiet place, we meet God's grace all alone.

MORNING
Go for It

When everything was hopeless, Abraham believed anyway,
deciding to live not on the basis of what he saw he couldn't
do but on what God said he would do.
ROMANS 4:18 MSG

This world is full of those who discourage rather than encourage.
If we believe them, we'll never do anything. But if we, like Abraham,
believe that God has called us for a particular purpose, we'll go for it
despite our track records. Past failure doesn't dictate future failure.
If God wills it, He fulfills it.

EVENING
Aim High

My aim is to raise hopes by
pointing the way to life without end.
TITUS 1:2 MSG

No woman is an island. We're more like peninsulas. Although we
sometimes feel isolated, we're connected to one another by the roots
of womanhood. We're all in this together, girls. As we look around, we
can't help but see sisters who need a hand, a warm smile, a caring touch.
And especially hope. People *need* hope, and if we know the Lord—
the source of eternal hope—it's up to us to point the way through love.

Morning
Awaken to Love

I will sing of your strength, in the morning I will sing of your love;
for you are my fortress, my refuge in times of trouble.
PSALM 59:16 NIV

Oh, the love of God! It's such a wonderful gift, pouring down from
the throne of God. Realizing His great love for us is overwhelming.
We can't help but praise! We find ourselves awakening in the
morning with songs of worship on our lips, thanking God for all
He's done for us. What an awesome way to start the day.

Evening
Encourage One Another

Not giving up meeting together, as some are in the habit of doing,
but encouraging one another—and all the more as
you see the Day approaching.
HEBREWS 10:25 NIV

Don't you love the encouragement you receive from your
brothers and sisters in Christ? They pour out God's love on you
and vice versa. Together the body of Christ is a force to be reckoned
with! And in these end times, we need each other more than ever!
With all of your heart, love your fellow believers.

MORNING
Limitless Joy

*"I have told you this so that my joy may be in
you and that your joy may be complete."*
JOHN 15:11 NIV

Did you realize that joy is limitless? It knows no boundaries. Jesus poured Himself out on the cross at Calvary giving everything so that you could experience fullness of joy. Even now, God longs to make Himself known to you in such a new and unique way. May you burst at the seams with this limitless joy as you enter His presence today.

EVENING
Giving Thanks

*"'There will be heard once more the sounds of joy and gladness,
the voices of bride and bridegroom, and the voices of those who bring thank
offerings to the house of the LORD, saying, "Give thanks to the LORD
Almighty, for the LORD is good; his love endures forever." For I will restore
the fortunes of the land as they were before,' says the LORD."*
JEREMIAH 33:10–11 NIV

One of the ways we "give" is to give thanks to the Lord. How easy it is to forget to thank Him for His many blessings. When we see His love for us, when we realize that He's never going to leave us or forsake us, we're motivated to give thanks. And as we lift our voices in praise, others are watching. We're teaching them to offer words of thanks to God, as well!

MORNING
Nothing More than Feelings

LORD, sustain me as you promised, that I may live!
Do not let my hope be crushed.
PSALM 119:116 NLT

Whatever our foe—unemployment, rejection, loss, illness—we may feel beaten down by life. Hope feels crushed by the relentless boulder bearing down on our souls. We feel that we can't possibly endure another day. Yes, we feel, we *feel*. But feelings are often deceiving. God promises to sustain us, to strengthen us, so that we might withstand that massive rock. We can trust Him. He will not allow us to be crushed!

EVENING
Praise Him!

The Lord is my strength, my song, and my salvation.
He is my God, and I will praise him.
EXODUS 15:2 TLB

God makes you strong; He makes you sing with gladness; and He rescues you from sin. These are the gifts of His grace. When He has given you so much, don't you want to give back to Him? Use your strength, your joy, and your freedom to praise Him.

MORNING

Open to Joy

"The joy of the LORD is your strength."
NEHEMIAH 8:10 NIV

Our God is a God of joy. He is not a God of sighing and gloom.
Open yourself to His joy. It is a gift of grace He longs to give you.
He knows it will make you strong.

EVENING

Jump In

You don't need more faith. There is no "more" or "less" in faith.
If you have a bare kernel of faith, say the size of a poppy seed, you could
say to this sycamore tree, "Go jump in the lake," and it would do it.
LUKE 17:6 MSG

Luke 17:6 is an intriguing verse. Jesus says there are no increments
of faith. You either have it or you don't. Just like you can't be just a
little pregnant—you either are or you aren't. Having the faith of Billy
Graham or Mother Teresa may seem unfathomable to us, but if we
earnestly and completely trust Jesus as our Savior, the Bible says we
already do. And God is ready to work through our lives as He has theirs.

MORNING
Spilling Over

And these things write we unto you,
that your joy may be full.
1 JOHN 1:4 KJV

Imagine you're in the process of filling a glass with water and accidentally pour too much in. The excess goes running down the sides, splashing your hand and anything else it comes in contact with. That's how it is when you're overflowing with joy from the inside out. You can't help but spill out onto others, and before long, they're touched, too. So, let it flow!

EVENING
Joined Together

Instead, speaking the truth in love, we will grow to become in every respect
the mature body of him who is the head, that is, Christ. From him the
whole body, joined and held together by every supporting ligament,
grows and builds itself up in love, as each part does its work.
EPHESIANS 4:15–16 NIV

Love graces us through our mistakes and joins us together as one body, the bride of Christ. We learn how to love by reading the Bible and spending time with God, who gave us the ultimate example of "how to" love when He sent His Son to die in our place. All He asks in return is that we give our hearts to Him. Go forth and love, dear friends!

MORNING
Tolerance Isn't Enough

"In his name the nations will put their hope."
MATTHEW 12:21 NIV

In the summer of 2000, my husband and I toured the Holy Land. Our Israeli guide assured us that there was no safer place than Jerusalem, for people of numerous faiths—Muslim, Jewish, Christian, Hindu—had learned tolerance as the key to living together peaceably. Yet tension was as evident as the armed guards on every street corner. Violence erupted three months later with the first bus bombings. Our only hope for peace is Jehovah.

EVENING
Abounding. . .More and More!

And it is my prayer that your love may abound more and more, with knowledge and all discernment, so that you may approve what is excellent, and so be pure and blameless for the day of Christ, filled with the fruit of righteousness that comes through Jesus Christ, to the glory and praise of God.
PHILIPPIANS 1:9–11 ESV

Have you ever watched a snowball roll down a hill? As it picks up speed, it begins to grow! Before long, it's huge and powerful! That's how love is. The more love you share, the more you get. The longer we love, the more we have the capacity to love. If you're hoping to receive more, try giving it away. Then get ready for the snowball effect!

MORNING
Harmony

*The hope of the [uncompromisingly] righteous (the upright,
in right standing with God) is gladness, but the expectation of
the wicked (those who are out of harmony with God) comes to nothing.*
PROVERBS 10:28 AMP

When we try to live our lives apart from God,
we put ourselves in a place where we can no longer see
His grace. Joy comes from being in harmony with God.

EVENING
Today—and Tomorrow

*You are my strong shield, and I trust you completely.
You have helped me, and I will celebrate and thank you in song.*
PSALM 28:7 CEV

God proves Himself to us over and over again. And yet over and over,
we doubt His power. We need to learn from experience. The God whose
strength rescued us yesterday and the day before will certainly rescue us
again today. As we celebrate the grace we received yesterday and the
day before, we gain confidence and faith for today and tomorrow.

MORNING
Shout for Joy!

Be glad in the LORD and rejoice, you righteous ones;
and shout for joy, all you who are upright in heart.
PSALM 32:11 NASB

Have you ever been so happy that you just felt like shouting? Ever been so overcome with joy that you wanted to holler your praise from the rooftops for all to hear? Well, what's holding you back? Go for it! Shout for joy! Let the whole world hear your praises to the King of kings!

EVENING
Integrity

Is not your fear of God your confidence,
and the integrity of your ways your hope?
JOB 4:6 NASB

Live your faith. These three little words are the goal of every Christian. *Not* "Don't smoke, cuss, or chew or hang around with those who do," or even "Be good so you'll get into heaven." Integrity begets behavior, not the other way around. We want to please our Lord by righteous behavior so we can fulfill the challenge of St. Francis of Assisi: "Preach the Gospel at all times. Use words if necessary."

Morning
Redeemed!

O Israel, hope in the Lord; for with the Lord there is lovingkindness,
and with Him is abundant redemption.
Psalm 130:7 nasb

The Psalmist knew Israel had a rotten track record. Throughout Old
Testament history, God miraculously delivered the Israelites from
trouble repeatedly, and they would gratefully turn to Him, only to
eventually slip again into rebellion and more trouble. Sounds a lot
like you and me, doesn't it? But thankfully, ours is a redemptive God;
a God who offers abundant lovingkindness and forgiveness.
A God of second chances—then and now.

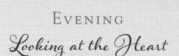

Evening
Looking at the Heart

"The Lord does not look at the things people look at.
People look at the outward appearance, but the Lord looks at the heart."
1 Samuel 16:7 niv

We tend to judge people by outward appearance, and sometimes
the way we treat them is affected, as well. Thankfully, God loves us
despite our spots and wrinkles! And He calls us to love others in spite
of any physical flaws. If you want to show the love of God to friends
or coworkers, don't judge them by what they wear, their hairstyles,
or their choice of makeup (or lack thereof). Just love them. Period.

MORNING
Into God's Presence

"That person can pray to God and find favor with him,
they will see God's face and shout for joy."
JOB 33:26 NIV

Prayer is the channel through which God's grace flows. We do not pray because God needs us to pray; we pray because *we* need to pray. When we come into God's presence, we are renewed. Our hearts lift. We look into the face of the One who loves us most, and we are filled with joy.

EVENING
Resting in His Abounding Love

"Come to me, all you who are weary and burdened, and I will give
you rest. Take my yoke upon you and learn from me, for I am
gentle and humble in heart, and you will find rest for your souls.
For my yoke is easy and my burden is light."
MATTHEW 11:28–31 NIV

If you're weary—exhausted with life—don't give up hope. God has a place of rest for those who are in relationship with Him. He woos us with His love, opening wide His arms and ushering us into His embrace. There we can hear His heartbeat. Get His perspective. Listen for His words of love, which energize us for the tasks ahead. Come, all you who are weary and heavy laden. Rest.

MORNING
Wanting Nothing

But let patience have its perfect work,
that you may be perfect and complete, lacking nothing.
JAMES 1:4 NKJV

Let patience have its perfect work? Ouch! It's hard enough to wait, even harder to wait patiently. Now we're supposed to let patience "work" in us while we're waiting? Sounds painful. . .and nearly impossible! But when we allow patience to have its perfect work in us, we are "complete," wanting nothing. We can wait patiently. . .and not stress about the yet-unanswered prayers. Every need is met in Him. Talk about joy!

EVENING
Strong in Christ

For I can do all things through
Christ who strengthens me.
PHILIPPIANS 4:13 NKJV

Left to ourselves, we are weak. We make mistakes. We fall short
of our goals. But in Christ, we are strong. By His grace,
we can accomplish anything.

MORNING
Mr. Clean for the Soul

As far as the east is from the west,
so far has He removed our transgressions from us.
PSALM 103:12 NASB

Dirty little secrets. We all have them. Exposing them is a popular theme for television shows these days. But we don't have to wallow in the muck of our past. God has promised to wash us clean of our dirty little secrets and remove them as far as the east is from the west when we repent of our wrongdoings and ask Him for forgiveness. An immaculate and sparkling fresh start—redemption is Mr. Clean for the soul!

EVENING
Glorious Awakening

I pray also that the eyes of your heart may be enlightened in
order that you may know the hope to which he has called you,
the riches of his glorious inheritance in his holy people.
EPHESIANS 1:18 NIV

"Open the eyes of my heart, Lord. I want to see you." The lyrics of this beautiful praise song express our deepest desire—to truly *see* the hope before us. Like stereograms with 3-D images embedded within 2-D pictures (You know, those hidden images you can't see without squinting?) the glory and riches of following Christ are veiled to some because the eyes of their hearts are closed. Let us pray for our own spiritual awakening today.

MORNING
Eternal Joy

You make known to me the path of life; you will fill me with
joy in your presence, with eternal pleasures at your right hand.
PSALM 16:11 NIV

God does not want you to be unhappy and confused. Believe in His
grace. He is waiting to show you the way to go. He is longing to give
you the joy of His presence. He wants to make you happy forever.

EVENING
Loving in Spite of Differences

But when the kindness and love of God our Savior appeared, he saved us,
not because of righteous things we had done, but because of his mercy.
He saved us through the washing of rebirth and renewal by the Holy Spirit.
TITUS 3:4–5 NIV

We're all different. All unique. God created us as individuals on
purpose! We have different philosophies, different political views,
and different ways of communicating. Thankfully, God's love supersedes
all of these differences. We are called to love in spite of them. Today,
instead of getting riled up at an acquaintance who sees things differently
than you do, extend love. It covers a multitude of differences.

MORNING
Rejoicing in Hope

[Be] rejoicing in hope; patient in tribulation;
continuing instant in prayer.
ROMANS 12:12 KJV

The words *rejoice* and *hope* just seem to go together, don't they? There's something about choosing joy that fills our hearts with hope for better days ahead. So what if we have to wait awhile? If we stay focused on the Lord, casting our cares on Him, that day of rejoicing will surely come!

EVENING
What God Requires

"And now, Israel, what does the LORD your God require of you,
but to fear the LORD your God, to walk in all his ways, to love him,
to serve the LORD your God with all your heart and with all your soul."
DEUTERONOMY 10:12 ESV

It's fascinating to think that God "requires" us to love Him. More interesting still is that it's listed in this scripture, along with walking in His ways, fearing Him, and serving Him. These things work well together, and all the more when love is tucked in the middle. First we fear (respect) God; then we show our love by obeying Him; and that leads to a life of service.

MORNING
Hit the Mats

Blessed are those whose help is the God of Jacob,
whose hope is in the LORD their God.
PSALM 146:5 NIV

Wrestled with God lately?
We all do at one time or another. The Genesis 32 account of Jacob's Almighty wrestling match reassures us that God is not offended when we beat on His chest and shout, "Why?" He understands that we must sometimes wrestle out the mysteries of our faith. Wrestling with his Lord was a turning point for Jacob—he got a new name (Israel) and a new perspective. God is ready to do the same for us.

EVENING
Lifted Up

But those who trust in the LORD will find new strength.
They will soar high on wings like eagles. They will run
and not grow weary. They will walk and not faint.
ISAIAH 40:31 NLT

Do you ever have days when you ask yourself, "How much further can I go? How much longer can I keep going like this?" On days like that, you long to give up. You wish you could just run away from the world and hide. Trust God's grace to give you the strength you need, even then. Let Him lift you up on eagle's wings.

MORNING
Shine!

The precepts of the LORD are right, giving joy to the heart.
The commands of the LORD are radiant, giving light to the eyes.
PSALM 19:8 NIV

As children, we probably felt sometimes as though rules had no purpose but to make us miserable. We didn't always understand that our parents' love was behind their rules. As adults, we often have the same attitude toward God's rules. We feel as though a life of sin might be easier, more fun. But instead, it's just the opposite. God always wants what will give us joy. His rules are designed to make us shine.

EVENING
Meet Me There

Christ gives me the strength to face anything.
PHILIPPIANS 4:13 CEV

Most women dread going out alone—to restaurants, shopping, social events—even church. Sometimes we are the loneliest when we're in a crowd. It's intimidating to face a roomful of strangers. But it's well worth it to bite the bullet and *just go* to that church brunch or spiritual retreat or Bible Study. I would have missed some awesome blessings if I hadn't gone (alone) to many spiritual events. I found I did know somebody after all. Jesus met me there.

MORNING

Joyous Tomorrow

But if we hope for that we see not,
then do we with patience wait for it.
ROMANS 8:25 KJV

Are you in a "waiting" season? Is your patience being tested to the breaking point? Take heart! You are not alone. Every godly man and woman from biblical times till now went through seasons of waiting on the Lord. Their secret? They hoped for what they could not see. (They never lost their hope!) And they waited patiently. So, as you're waiting, reflect on the biblical giants and realize. . .you're not alone!

EVENING

Worship Styles

For in Christ Jesus neither circumcision nor uncircumcision
counts for anything, but only faith working through love.
GALATIANS 5:6 ESV

The body of Christ is made up of millions of people around the globe. We're like snowflakes. No two of us are alike. Sure, we praise the same God, but we worship differently. Some praise with great enthusiasm. Others prefer a quiet, peaceful worship service. Instead of focusing on our differences, love sees past them and strives for unity. What is the one force that unites us? Jesus! And Jesus is love.

Morning
BFF

I am counting on the LORD; yes, I am counting on him.
I have put my hope in his word.
PSALM 130:5 NLT

"Best Friends Forever" earn this title of honor because we've learned
we can count on them. They've proven they'll be there for us through
svelte and bloated, sweet and grumpy, thoughtful and insensitive.
Bailing us out of countless sinking dinghies, they've held us as we
sobbed, fed our families, watched our kids, and made us smile.
How much more can we count on our Creator to be there for us?

Evening
Keep His Word

Jesus answered him, "If anyone loves me, he will keep my word,
and my Father will love him, and we will come to him and make our
home with him. Whoever does not love me does not keep my words.
And the word that you hear is not mine but the Father's who sent me."
JOHN 14:23–24 ESV

Love and obedience have always walked hand in hand. If we love God,
we will obey Him. Sure, our flesh doesn't always want to do it, but we'll
have the best outcome if we stick with the teachings of the Bible and
follow God's precepts to the best of our ability. Love equals obedience.

MORNING
What God Shows Us

The LORD is righteous in everything he does;
he is filled with kindness.
PSALM 145:17 NLT

Did you know that the word *kind* comes from the same root as *kin*?
Both words originally had to do with intimate shared relationships
like the ones that exist between members of the same family. This is
what God shows us: the kindness of a good father, the gentleness
of a good mother, the understanding of a brother or sister.

EVENING
Where Credit Is Due

It is not that we think we are qualified to do anything on our own.
Our qualification comes from God.
2 CORINTHIANS 3:5 NLT

It's easy to seek God when we feel like failures, but when success
comes our way, we like to congratulate ourselves rather than give
God the credit. When we achieve great things, we need to remember
that it is God's grace through us that brought about our success.

MORNING
Approaching the Throne with Joy

In every prayer of mine I always make my entreaty
and petition for you all with joy (delight).
PHILIPPIANS 1:4 AMP

Sometimes we approach our prayer time with God with a list in hand,
much like a child at Christmastime. Other times we approach the Lord
with fear leading the way. "What happens if He doesn't respond like I
hope?" Though we don't need to come with a Christmas list in hand,
we do need to confidently approach our heavenly Father and make
our requests with joy. He loves us, after all! So, draw near!

EVENING
Fly Me Away

But those who hope in the LORD will renew their strength.
They will soar on wings like eagles; they will run and
not grow weary, they will walk and not be faint.
ISAIAH 40:31 NIV

On those weary days when our chins drag the ground, when our feet
are stuck fast in the quagmire of everyday responsibility, this verse
becomes our hope and our prayer: Mount me up with wings like eagles;
Father, fly me away! Let my spirit soar above the clouds on the winds
of your strength. Make me strong as a marathon runner, continuing
mile after mile after mile. Be my tailwind, Lord. Amen.

MORNING
Heaven's Bakery

Those who hope in me will not be disappointed.
ISAIAH 49:23 NIV

As I stood in line ogling luscious pastries in the coffee shop's glass case, I asked the teenage clerk which she would suggest. Casting cornflower-blue eyes heavenward, she tapped her dainty chin with one finger before answering in a wistful voice. "I recommend the blueberry cheesecake. When I eat it, I hear angels." What higher recommendation is there? What greater hope have we than heaven? (Maybe they'll even serve blueberry cheesecake there!)

EVENING
From Everlasting to Everlasting

But from everlasting to everlasting the LORD's love is with those who fear him, and his righteousness with their children's children.
PSALM 103:17 NIV

Isn't it interesting to think that God has existed forever? Before He created the heavens and the earth, He was. And He will be here in the "forever" yet to come, as well. Even more amazing, God has been in love with His people forever. He loved humankind in the garden, and He will love us long after we're all in heaven with Him. His love truly reaches from everlasting to everlasting.

MORNING
Rope of Love

*"I led them with cords of human kindness, with ropes of love.
I lifted the yoke from their neck and bent down and fed them."*
HOSEA 11:4 NCV

God's grace is not a lasso looped around our shoulders, trapping us
and binding us tight. Instead, grace reaches out to us through the
kindness of others. It is a rope of love that stretches through
our lives, leading us to freedom.

EVENING
God Keeps His Covenant

*"Understand, therefore, that the LORD your God is indeed God. He is the
faithful God who keeps his covenant for a thousand generations and lavishes
his unfailing love on those who love him and obey his commands."*
DEUTERONOMY 7:9 NLT

A covenant is an agreement between two parties. Sure, we sign on
the dotted line—or shake hands on a matter—but we don't always
follow through. Not so with God. He always follows through on His
agreement, even when we fall short. And He continues to lavish us with
His unfailing love when we love Him back and obey His commands.

MORNING
Continued Prayers

Continue in prayer, and watch in the same with thanksgiving.
COLOSSIANS 4:2 KJV

Are you the sort of person who gives up easily? Does your faith waver if God doesn't respond to your prayers right away? Don't give up, and don't stop praying, particularly if you're believing God for something that seems impossible. Be like that little widow woman in the Bible. . . the one who pestered the judge until he responded. Just keep at it. As you continue in prayer, keep a joyful heart, filled with expectation.

EVENING
Careful Plans

Without good advice everything goes wrong—
it takes careful planning for things to go right.
PROVERBS 15:22 CEV

The Bible reminds us that when we start a new venture, we should not trust success to come automatically. We need to seek out the advice of those we trust. We need to make careful plans. And most of all, we need to seek God's counsel, praying for the grace and wisdom to do things right.

MORNING
Beyond the Horizon

Always continue to fear the LORD. You will be rewarded for this;
your hope will not be disappointed.
PROVERBS 23:17–18 NLT

Have you ever traversed a long, winding road, unable to see your
final destination? Perhaps you were surprised by twists and turns
along the way or jarred by unexpected potholes. But you were
confident that if you stayed on *that* road, you would eventually
reach your destination. Likewise, God has mapped out our futures.
The end of the road may disappear beyond the horizon, but we are
assured that our destination will not be disappointing.

EVENING
Fill 'Er Up

What strength do I have, that I should still hope?
JOB 6:11 NIV

Run, rush, hurry, dash: a typical American woman's day. It's easy to
identify with David's lament in Psalm 22:14 (NASB): "I am poured out
like water. . .my heart is like wax; it is melted within me." Translation:
I'm pooped; I'm numb; I'm drained dry. When we are at the end of
our strength, God doesn't want us to lose hope of the refilling He
can provide if we only lift our empty cups to Him.

MORNING
Freely Given

Out of sheer generosity he put us in right standing with himself.
A pure gift. He got us out of the mess we're in and restored us to where
he always wanted us to be. And he did it by means of Jesus Christ.
ROMANS 3:24 MSG

How kind God has been to us! He brought us close to Himself. He reached down and picked us up out of our messy lives. He healed us so we could be the people we were always meant to be. That is what grace is: a gift we never deserved, freely given out of love.

EVENING
Drawn with Loving-Kindness

"I have loved you with an everlasting love;
I have drawn you with unfailing kindness."
JEREMIAH 31:3 NIV

"Infinity" is a difficult concept to grasp. When we say the word *forever*, we're keenly aware that the forever life goes far beyond what we experience here on earth. When we ask Jesus to come into our hearts and He becomes Lord of our lives, we step into a "forever" existence with Him. And His love lasts forever, too. It's not just meant for the here and now, but for all eternity. Praise God for His everlasting love!

Morning

Enjoying Life

*Let all who seek You rejoice and be glad in You; and let those
who love Your salvation say continually, "Let God be magnified."
. . .You are my help and my deliverer.*
PSALM 70:4–5 NASB

Sometimes we approach God robotically: "Lord, please do this for me.
Lord, please do that." We're convinced we'll be happy, if only
God grants our wishes, like a genie in a bottle. We're going about
this backward! We should start by praising God. Thank Him for
life, health, and the many answered prayers. Our joyous praise will
remind us just how blessed we already are! Then out of genuine
relationship we make our requests known.

Evening

Balance

*She gets up before dawn to prepare breakfast for her
household and plan the day's work for her servant girls.*
PROVERBS 31:15 NLT

You've got a lot to do. Each of your roles shouts for attention. How can
you do it all? You can't. You're only one woman, although a caring,
capable one. As a new employee, first-time mother, or start-up
business owner, you encounter huge learning curves. You'll need
to make adjustments. You may need to wake up early or ask for
specialized help. This phase won't last forever. Give yourself a break.
Do what you need to do to maintain balance.

MORNING
I Do

Let us hold unswervingly to the hope we profess,
for he who promised is faithful.
HEBREWS 10:23 NIV

An important part of any marriage is the vow of faithfulness.
We pledge that we will remain faithful to our beloved until death do
us part. Faithfulness is *crucial* to a trusting relationship. We must be
able to depend on our spouse to always be in our corner, love us even
when we're unlovable, and never leave or forsake us. God is faithful.
We can unswervingly depend on Him to never break His promises.

EVENING
Wonderful!

Commit your actions to the LORD,
and your plans will succeed.
PROVERBS 16:3 NLT

Just because we *want* something to happen, doesn't mean it will,
no matter how hard we pray. We've all found that out (often to
our sorrow!). But when we truly commit everything we do to God,
praying only for His grace to be given free rein in our lives, then we
will be surprised by what comes about. It may not be what
we imagined—but it will be wonderful!

MORNING

Choose Grace

*And a servant of the Lord must not quarrel but
must be kind to everyone, a good teacher, and patient.*
2 TIMOTHY 2:24 NCV

Some days we can't help but feel irritated and out of sorts. But no matter how we feel on the inside, we can choose our outward behavior. We can make the decision to let disagreements go, to refuse to argue, to act in kindness, to show patience and a willingness to listen (even when we *feel* impatient). We can choose to walk in grace.

EVENING

Reboot

Be strong in the Lord and in his mighty power.
EPHESIANS 6:10 NLT

The toilet overflows, sink regurgitates, check bounces, temper flies, washing machine dances, scale shows a three pound *gain*, kids stampede, husband forgets *again*. . . . Ever have one of those days? You're at the end of your rope, barely hanging on with clawed fingernails. How marvelous that when we're at our weakest point, our Lord is at His strongest, and He gladly shares that strength with us. He won't necessarily fix the plumbing or rewire the spouse, but He *will* reboot our attitudes.

MORNING
Daily Provision

*"Who provides food for the raven when its young cry
out to God and wander about for lack of food?"*
JOB 38:41 NIV

Does it fill your heart with joy to know that God provides for your
needs? He makes provision. . .both in seasons of want and seasons of
plenty. There's no need to strive. No need to worry. He's got it all under
control. If He provides food for the ravens, then surely He knows how
to give you everything you need when you need it. So, praise Him!

EVENING
Flourishing in God's Love

*But I am like an olive tree flourishing in the house of God;
I trust in God's unfailing love for ever and ever.*
PSALM 52:8 NIV

When we trust in God's unfailing, everlasting love, we flourish like trees
planted by streams of living water. We continue to grow and thrive.
As you ponder this "forever" love that God offers through His Son,
trust that He will walk you through the rest of your days stronger
than you've ever been. You can flourish in God's everlasting love!

MORNING
Can You Hear Me Now?

But as for me, I watch in hope for the LORD,
I wait for God my Savior; my God will hear me.
MICAH 7:7 NIV

If there's anything more frustrating than waiting for someone who never shows, it's trying to talk to someone who isn't listening. It's as if they have plugged their ears and nothing penetrates. Mothers are well acquainted with this exercise in futility, as are wives, daughters, and sisters. But the Bible tells us that God hears us when we talk to Him. He shows up when we wait for Him. He will not disappoint us.

EVENING
Beauty

She'll garland your life with grace,
she'll festoon your days with beauty.
PROVERBS 4:9 MSG

You are a beautiful creation of God. As a woman with a heart for God, you seek wisdom and understanding, and it shows. Grace reflects in your eyes as you speak with kindness and encouragement. Magazine advertisements and Hollywood may tell you that to be one of the "beautiful people" you must maintain an ideal weight, banish wrinkles, schedule regular pedicures, highlight your hair—and more. While all these regimens are fine, wisdom's loveliness in you far exceeds them all.

MORNING
Laugh Out Loud

*"He will once again fill your mouth with
laughter and your lips with shouts of joy."*
JOB 8:21 NLT

Did you know that God wants to make you laugh? He wants to
fill you with loud, rowdy joy. Oh, some days His grace will
come to you quietly and calmly. But every now and then,
you will have days when He makes you laugh out loud.

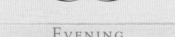

EVENING
Whatever Comes Next

*"You will succeed in whatever you choose to do,
and light will shine on the road ahead of you."*
JOB 22:28 NLT

The word *success* originally meant simply "the thing that comes
next." Over the years, we've added to that meaning the sense that
success has to be the thing we wanted to happen, the outcome for
which we hoped. But God does not necessarily define success the
way we do. Whatever comes next, no matter what, His grace
transforms it, using circumstances to create the light we need
to travel still further on our road to heaven.

MORNING

Joyous Provision

And my God will meet all your needs
according to the riches of his glory in Christ Jesus.
PHILIPPIANS 4:19 NIV

Sometimes God goes overboard when it's time to make provision.
He blesses us above and beyond what we could ask or think.
He not only meets our needs. . .He throws in a bit of excess,
just to watch us smile. If you're in a season of abundant provision,
remember to share the joy! Pass on a portion of what He has
given you. And praise Him! What an awesome God we serve!

EVENING

Fearfully Made

You knit me together in my mother's womb.
I praise you because I am fearfully and wonderfully made.
PSALM 139:13–14 NIV

Crow's feet, frizzy hair, saddle bags, big feet—most women dislike
something about their bodies. We feel much more fearfully than
wonderfully made. But God loves us just as we are. He wants us to look
past the wrinkles and see laugh footprints; to use those knobby knees
for praying and age-spotted hands for serving. And in the process, praise
Him for limbs that move, eyes that see, and ears that hear His Word.

MORNING
Pure and Unspoiled

*And everyone who has this hope fixed on
Him purifies himself, just as He is pure.*
1 JOHN 3:3 NASB

Don't you just love taking the first scoop of ice cream from a fresh half-gallon? There's something about the smooth surface of unspoiled purity that satisfies the soul. It's the same with new jars of peanut butter, freshly fallen snow, or stretches of pristine, early morning beach sand. God looks at us that way—unblemished, pure and unspoiled—through our faith and hope in Him. Allow that thought to bring a smile to your face today.

EVENING
I Hope in Him

*The Lord's love never ends; his mercies never stop.
They are new every morning; LORD, your loyalty is great.
I say to myself, "The LORD is mine, so I hope in him."*
LAMENTATIONS 3:22–24 NCV

God's love is steadfast. Steady. Unwavering. It isn't tossed about by every wind, blown here and there. When we love others, our feelings sometimes shift. We're hot one day, cold the next. Not so with the Lord. He's in it for the long haul, even when we mess up. And this steadfast love keeps us through this life and the life to come. All praise to the One whose mercies never come to an end!

MORNING

Transformed

And Sarah declared, "God has brought me laughter.
All who hear about this will laugh with me."
GENESIS 21:6 NLT

The first time we read of Sarah laughing, it was because she doubted
God. She didn't believe that at her age she would have a baby.
But God didn't hold her laughter against her. Instead, He transformed
it. He turned her laughter of scorn and doubt into the
laughter of fulfillment and grace.

EVENING

Blessing

The blessing of the LORD makes one rich.
PROVERBS 10:22 NKJV

God blesses His children. No doubt about it. Just look around you.
Your life is richer because of His protection, provision, presence,
grace, and love. How can you respond to God's blessing? Gratefully
accept Him and all that He gives you. And then bless Him back.
Perhaps that seems like the ultimate audacity. The perfect Bless-er
receiving blessings from His own creation? Yet out of your rich inner
resources of blessing, you can honor, revere, and bless the Giver.

MORNING
Who Provides?

Consider the lilies how they grow:
they toil not, they spin not.
LUKE 12:27 KJV

Sometimes we look at our job as our provision. We say things like, "I work for my money." While it's true that we work hard (and are rewarded with a paycheck) we can't forget that God is our provider. If He cares for the lilies of the field—flowers that bloom for such a short season—then how much more does He care for us, His children? What joy. . .realizing God loves us enough to provide for our needs.

EVENING
Vehicle for God's Grace

Do not neglect your gift. . . . Be diligent in these matters;
give yourself wholly to them, so that everyone may see your progress.
1 TIMOTHY 4:14–15 NIV

God expects us to use the talents He gave us. Don't turn away from them with a false sense of modesty. Exercise them. Improve your skills. Whatever your gift may be, use it as a vehicle for God's grace.

MORNING
Unfathomable Grace

Jesus treated us much better than we deserve.
He made us acceptable to God and gave us the hope of eternal life.
TITUS 3:7 CEV

Whereas justice is getting what we deserve and mercy is *not* getting what we deserve, grace is getting what we *don't* deserve. Thankfully, God doesn't automatically dole out justice for our myriad sins, but reaches beyond to mercy and even a step further to grace. As Jean Valjean discovers in the classic story, *Les Misérables*, when we truly grasp God's unfathomable mercy and grace, we are then empowered to extend it to others.

EVENING
All in the Family

We are God's house, if we keep our courage
and remain confident in our hope in Christ.
HEBREWS 3:6 NLT

Just as our children gain their identity from being an integral part of our household, we proudly bear the identity of our Father's house. What an honor! To be a member of God's household! To even take out the garbage or clean our rooms is a privilege.

MORNING
Witness of Laughter

We were filled with laughter, and we sang for joy. And the other nations said, "What amazing things the LORD has done for them."
PSALM 126:2 NLT

Life is truly amazing. Each day, grace touches us in many ways, from the sun on our faces to each person we meet, from the love of our friends and families to the satisfaction of our work. Pay attention. Let people hear you laugh more. Don't hide your joy. It's a witness to God's love.

EVENING
Glory Forever and Ever

To him who loves us and has freed us from our sins by his blood, and has made us to be a kingdom and priests to serve his God and Father— to him be glory and power for ever and ever! Amen.
REVELATION 1:5–6 NIV

Oh, how the love of God propels us to praise! His everlasting love has saved us, freed us, and made us His heirs, His children, His own. There's no other place we can go to receive such unconditional love. May we continue to worship Him from now until eternity, offering praise and glory for this spectacular love!

MORNING
Joyfully Satisfied

"I will abundantly bless her provision;
I will satisfy her needy with bread."
PSALM 132:15 NASB

The Lord has promised to meet all of our needs, according to His riches in glory. His heart is for His people, especially the poor and downtrodden. Today, as you seek God about your own needs, ask Him how you can help meet the needs of the less fortunate in your community. What a joy it will be, to reach out to others. . . even if you're also in need.

EVENING
Boundaries

I, Wisdom, live together with good judgment. . . . I was there when he
set the limits of the seas, so they would not spread beyond their boundaries.
PROVERBS 8:12, 29 NLT

Wisdom originates with God. When God designed the world, wisdom watched with joy as He drew distinct boundaries around the oceans and seas to protect His other creation from drowning. It's a picture of the boundaries He designed for you. You are not your mother. You are not your friend. You are not your spouse. No one has a right to step over your boundary line and take advantage of you. You are distinct. God made you that way.

Morning
Roll Down the Window

Ask and it will be given to you; seek and you will find;
knock and the door will be opened to you.

LUKE 11:9 NIV

Does your fellow have trouble asking directions? Do you cruise about the country on a scenic tour that could have been avoided by asking a simple question? We all find it difficult to some degree when it comes to asking for help. But that's how we reach our final destinations—and not just on the highway. God offers help if we only ask. He's standing there holding the road map. We just have to stop and roll down the window.

Evening
From God

There are different kinds of gifts,
but they are all from the same Spirit.

1 CORINTHIANS 12:4 NCV

God shines through us in different ways. One person is good at expressing herself in words; another is good with children; and still another has a gift for giving wise counsel to her friends. Whatever our gifts are, they all come from God. They are all tangible expressions of His grace.

Morning
Trust Him

You people who are now crying are blessed,
because you will laugh with joy.
LUKE 6:21 NCV

God's grace comes to you even in the midst of tears. He is there with you in your hurt and your sadness. Trust in Him, knowing that sadness does not last forever. One day you will laugh again.

Evening
Send Me a Sign

Let your unfailing love surround us,
LORD, for our hope is in you alone.
PSALM 33:22 NLT

With deadlines and schedules swirling in my head while driving down the interstate, I did a double take at the car passing me. A white-painted message across the back passenger window grabbed my attention: I AM LOVED. Wow. So am I. It took only a moment to thank Papa God for His unfailing love, but a smile lit my face all day. A simple but profound reminder is all we need from time to time.

MORNING
Joy in Heaven

*"In the same way, there is more joy in heaven over one lost
sinner who repents and returns to God than over ninety-nine
others who are righteous and haven't strayed away!"*
LUKE 15:7 NLT

What a party heaven throws when one person comes to know the Lord!
Can't you see it now? The angels let out a shout! The trumpeters
play their victory chant. All of heaven reacts joyfully to the news.
Oh, that we would respond with such joy to the news of a lost
soul turning to the Lord. What a celebration!

EVENING
An Anxious Heart

*A miserable heart means a miserable life;
a cheerful heart fills the day with song.*
PROVERBS 15:15 MSG

Have you ever felt weighted down? Heavy? Sometimes the cares
of this life can make us so anxious that we see only the tips of our
toes, not the road ahead. Today, lift your eyes! Speak words of faith
and hope over your situation. Go out of your way to cheer someone
else up. This simple act will lift your spirits and cause you to forget
about your own burdens. Watch the joy sweep in!

MORNING

Cherished Desire

*God our Father loves us. He is kind and has
given us eternal comfort and a wonderful hope.*
2 THESSALONIANS 2:16 CEV

Webster's definition of *hope*: "to cherish a desire with expectation."
In other words, yearning for something wonderful you *expect* to occur.
Our hope in Christ is not just yearning for something wonderful,
as in "I hope for a sunny beach day." It's a deep trust with roots that
extend from the beginning of time to the infinite future. Our hope is
not just the anticipation of heaven, but the expectation of a fulfilling
life walking beside our Creator and best Friend.

EVENING

Busyness

The diligent find freedom in their work.
PROVERBS 12:24 MSG

It's fun watching a juggler. He tosses and balances balls, knives, hats,
and sometimes flaming torches. It appears easy. Yet if you asked, you'd
probably discover how many focused and diligent hours he practices.
Learning to work without the constant buzz of busyness is like learning
a juggling act. Although you want to stop rushing, it feels so impossible
that you're tempted to cease trying. But be encouraged. You'll find
success if you stay committed to practicing a balanced schedule.

Morning
Full!

"I came that they may have and enjoy life,
and have it in abundance (to the full, till it overflows)."

JOHN 10:10 AMP

The life we have in Christ is not restricted or narrow. Grace doesn't flow
to us in a meager trickle; it fills our life to the fullest. God's grace comes
to us each moment, day after day, year after year, a generous flood that
fills every crack and crevice of our lives—and then overflows.

Evening
Creative Expression

Not only has the LORD filled him with his Spirit, but he has given
him wisdom and made him a skilled craftsman who can create
objects of art with gold, silver, bronze, stone, and wood.

EXODUS 35:31 CEV

We were designed to be creative people. Whether we sew clothes
or paint pictures, come up with new business ideas or write stories,
make a welcoming home or cook delicious meals, God's creativity
longs to be expressed through us. As we exercise our creative talents,
we are united with Him. His Spirit works through our hands, creating
visions of grace as we make the world a lovelier place for us all.

MORNING

Rejoicing in Salvation

Then my soul will rejoice in the LORD
and delight in his salvation.

PSALM 35:9 NIV

Do you remember what it felt like to put your trust in Christ for the first time? Likely, you've never experienced anything else that brought such joy, such release. Oh, the joy of that salvation experience. The overwhelming realization that the God of the universe loves you enough to send His only Son to die on a cross so that you could have eternal life. There's no greater joy than the joy of salvation.

EVENING

No Greater Comfort

"O death, where is your victory?
O death, where is your sting?"

1 CORINTHIANS 15:55 NASB

There's no denying that the loss of a loved one stings. Our hearts burn, sear, and ache with pain. But Christ's victory over death after His crucifixion enables His followers to experience that same victory. We, too, will stand as conquerors of the grave, arm in arm with believers who have gone before us. What greater hope? What greater comfort?

MORNING
Seeking an Oasis

He changes a wilderness into a pool of
water and a dry land into springs of water.
PSALM 107:35 NASB

The wilderness of Israel is truly a barren wasteland—nothing but
rocks and parched sand stretching as far as the distant horizon.
The life-and-death contrast between stark desert and pools of oasis
water is startling. Our lives can feel parched, too. Colorless. Devoid of life.
But God has the power to transform desert lives into gurgling, spring-of-
water lives. Ask Him to bubble up springs of hope within you today.

EVENING
Thou Shalt Not Worry!

"Do not worry about tomorrow, for tomorrow will worry about itself.
Each day has enough trouble of its own."
MATTHEW 6:34 NIV

What if the Lord had written an eleventh commandment:
"Thou shalt not worry"? In a sense, He did! He commands us in
various scriptures not to fret. So, cast your anxieties on the Lord.
Give them up! Let them go! Don't let worries zap your strength
and your joy. Today is a gift from the Lord. Don't sacrifice it to fears
and frustrations! Let them go. . .and watch God work!

MORNING
Sing!

But each day the LORD pours his unfailing love upon me,
and through each night I sing his songs, praying to God who gives me life.
PSALM 42:8 NLT

Life itself is a gift of grace. The very blood that flows through our veins, the beat of our hearts, and the steady hum of our metabolism—all of that is God's free gift to us, a token of His constant and unconditional love. When we are so richly loved, how can we help but sing, even in the darkness?

EVENING
Calmness

Foolish people lose their tempers,
but wise people control theirs.
PROVERBS 29:11 NCV

Feeling angry doesn't automatically mean you've sinned. Anger is a normal response to injustice and wrong. God becomes angry over the disobedience of the people He loves. Jesus responded angrily to the corrupt money changers in the temple, but He didn't sin. It's when anger is allowed to rage or fester as resentment that it wreaks havoc with your soul and relationships. You're wise when you face your anger responsibly, discover its roots, and partner with God to control it.

MORNING
Restored Joy

Restore unto me the joy of thy salvation;
and uphold me with thy free spirit.
PSALM 51:12 KJV

When you restore your home, you return it to its prior state, its best possible condition. But is it possible to restore joy? Can you really get it back once lost? Of course you can! Joy is a choice and can be restored with a single decision. Decide today. Make up your mind. Get ready for the renovation to take place as you ask the Lord to restore the joy of your salvation.

EVENING
Use Your Gift

Each of you has been blessed with one of God's many wonderful
gifts to be used in the service of others. So use your gift well.
1 PETER 4:10 CEV

God did not give you your talents for your own pleasure only. These skills you have were meant to be offered to the world. He wants to use them to build His kingdom here on earth. So pick up your skill, whatever it is, and use it to bring grace to someone's life.

MORNING
Name Above All Names

*O God, we give glory to you all day long
and constantly praise your name.*
PSALM 44:8 NLT

So what has God done that deserves our everlasting praise?
His descriptive names tell the story: A friend that sticks closer than a
brother (Proverbs 18:24), Altogether lovely (Song of Solomon 5:16),
The rock that is higher than I (Psalm 61:2), My strength and my
song (Isaiah 12:2), The lifter of my head (Psalm 3:3), Shade from
the heat (Isaiah 25:4). His very name fills us with hope!

EVENING
Laugh a Rainbow

*When I see the rainbow in the clouds, I will remember the eternal
covenant between God and every living creature on earth.*
GENESIS 9:16 NLT

Ever feel like a cloud is hanging over your head? Sometimes the cloud
darkens to the color of bruises, and we're deluged with cold rain
that seems to have no end. When you're in the midst of one of life's
thunderstorms, tape this saying to your mirror: *cry a river, laugh a
rainbow*. The rainbow, the symbol of hope that God gave Noah after
the flood, reminds us even today that every storm will eventually pass.

MORNING
Surrender

"For whoever wants to save their life will lose it,
but whoever loses their life for me will save it."
LUKE 9:24 NIV

Life is full of paradoxes. God seems to delight in turning our
ideas inside out and backward. It doesn't seem to make sense,
but the only way to possess our life is to surrender it absolutely
into God's hands. As we let go of everything, God's grace
gives everything back to us, transformed by His love.

EVENING
Anxious Striving

What do people get for all the toil and anxious
striving with which they labor under the sun?
ECCLESIASTES 2:22 NIV

Sometimes, out of anxiety, we bury ourselves in work. We labor from
sunup till sundown. There's nothing wrong with working hard, but
striving is another thing altogether. When we "strive," we're not trusting
God to do His part. We're taking matters into our own hands. Today,
take a moment to ask yourself an important question: "Am I working,
or am I striving?" Don't let the enemy steal your joy! Strive no more!

MORNING
The Rock of Our Salvation

O come, let us sing unto the LORD:
let us make a joyful noise to the rock of our salvation.
PSALM 95:1 KJV

God never changes. He's the same yesterday, today, and forever. We go through a multitude of changes in our lives, but, praise God, He's consistent. Doesn't that bring joy to your heart, to realize that the Creator of the universe is our Rock? And don't you feel like celebrating when you realize that, no matter how much you mess up, His promise of salvation is true? Praise be to the Lord, our Rock!

EVENING
Character

Good character is the best insurance.
PROVERBS 11:6 MSG

You can't know the future—even what will happen an hour from now. So you do what you can to protect yourself and your family and then give your tomorrows to God. Some things are not within your control. Yet it is always within your power to grow spiritually. You can choose to pray, read God's Word, and listen to His Spirit's gentle direction. As you do, you'll learn who He is and He'll graciously develop love, patience, gentleness, and wisdom in you.

MORNING
First Love

But you must stay deeply rooted and firm in your faith.
You must not give up the hope you received when you heard the good news.
COLOSSIANS 1:23 CEV

Do you remember the day you turned your life over to Christ? Can you recall the flood of joy and hope that coursed through your veins? Ah, the wonder of first love. Like romantic love that deepens and broadens with passing years, our relationship with Jesus evolves into a river of faith that endures the test of time.

EVENING
Outside of Time's Stream

Your throne, O LORD, has stood from time immemorial.
You yourself are from the everlasting past.
PSALM 93:2 NLT

If you think of time as a fast-moving river, then we are creatures caught in its stream, thrust ever forward into the future, while the past rushes away behind us. Life keeps slipping away from us like water between our fingers. But God is outside of time's stream. He holds our past safely in His hands, and His grace is permanent and unshakable. His love is the lifesaver to which we cling in the midst of time's wild waves.

MORNING
Radiant

"If you are filled with light, with no dark corners, then your whole life will be radiant, as though a floodlight were filling you with light."
LUKE 11:36 NLT

We all have dark corners in our lives we keep hidden. We hide them from others. We hide them from God, and we even try to hide them from ourselves. But God wants to shine His light even into our darkest, most private nooks and crannies. He wants us to step out into the floodlight of His love—and then His grace will make us shine.

EVENING
Asking Why?

God will never forget the needy;
the hope of the afflicted will never perish.
PSALM 9:18 NIV

Why me? Why is God allowing this to happen? Why doesn't He intervene? When we're in the midst of a difficult time, it's easy to forget that God is not the *afflicter*, but is the helper and healer of the *afflicted*. He is not cracking the whip, but feels every stripe inflicted on our backs by a sin-filled world—just like those of His only Son, Jesus.

MORNING
A Compassionate Heart

Break forth into joy, sing together, you waste places of Jerusalem!
For the LORD has comforted His people, He has redeemed Jerusalem.
ISAIAH 52:9 NKJV

Have you ever knelt to comfort a child as the tears flowed down his or her little cheeks? If so, then you understand the heart of your Daddy God as He gently wipes away your tears during times of sorrow. He comforts as only a Father can, bringing hope where there is no hope and joy where there is no joy. What a compassionate God we serve!

EVENING
Bubbling Joy

Can both fresh water and salt water flow from the same spring?
JAMES 3:11 NIV

Can you feel it. . .that bubbling in your midsection? Can you sense it rising to the surface? Joy comes from the deepest place inside of us, so deep that we often forget it's there at all. Wonder of wonders! It rises up, up, up to the surface and the most delightful thing happens. Troubles vanish. Sorrows disappear. Godly joy has the power to squelch negative emotions. So, let the bubbling begin!

MORNING
Feel the Love

Long before he laid down earth's foundations, he had us in mind, had settled
on us as the focus of his love, to be made whole and holy by his love.
EPHESIANS 1:4 MSG

Need a boost of hope today? Read this passage aloud, inserting your
name for each "us." Wow! Doesn't that bring home the message of
God's incredible, extravagant, customized love for you? I am the *focus*
of His love, and I bask in the hope of healing, wholeness, and holiness
His individualized attention brings. You, too, dear sister, are His focus.
Allow yourself to feel the love today.

EVENING
Commitment

Commit your works to the LORD,
and your thoughts will be established.
PROVERBS 16:3 NKJV

When you don't understand all that's happening and aren't certain what
to do next, honor your initial commitment to God. Continue with what
God has shown you in the light or in less confusing times. Do what is
in front of you to do—without retreating into an isolating fear-maze.
Although you may not know what your long-term future holds, walk
through the doors of opportunity that open each day. In time God
will establish your thoughts and clarify your path.

MORNING

Love Is Bigger

> *"Love the LORD your God with all your heart*
> *and with all your soul and with all your might."*
> DEUTERONOMY 6:5 NASB

Love is not merely a feeling. It's far bigger than that. Love fills
up our emotions, but it also fills our thoughts. Our body's strength
and energy feed it. It requires discipline and determination.
Loving God requires the effort of our whole being.

EVENING

Meant to Move

> *We are only foreigners living here on earth for a while, just as our ancestors*
> *were. And we will soon be gone, like a shadow that suddenly disappears.*
> 1 CHRONICLES 29:15 CEV

We are not meant to feel too at home in this world. Maybe that is why
time is designed to keep us from lingering too long in one place. We are
meant to be moving on, making our way to our forever-home in heaven.
Grace has brought us safe thus far—and grace will lead us home.

MORNING

Sorrows. . .Be Gone!

*"Very truly I tell you, you will weep and mourn while the world rejoices.
You will grieve, but your grief will turn to joy."*
JOHN 16:20 NIV

Imagine you're washing a load of white towels. One of them is badly
stained. You add bleach to the wash load and let it run its cycle.
Afterward, you can't tell which towel is which! The same is true when
we allow God to wash away our sorrows. When all is said and done, all
that remains is the joy!

EVENING

Tune In

*And hope does not put us to shame, because God's love has been poured out
into our hearts through the Holy Spirit, who has been given to us.*
ROMANS 5:5 NIV

Is your spiritual antenna tuned in to the Holy Spirit? The Holy
Spirit is the communicator of the Trinity: our helper, comforter,
and instructor. Through Him, God pours love and hope into us.
Like radio waves broadcasting invisibly through the atmosphere,
the Holy Spirit communicates to believers. We must, however,
make the effort to tune in our receivers to His frequency, and
then choose to *obey* His guidance—even when it's inconvenient.

MORNING
Forever and Always

"Never will I leave you; never will I forsake you."
HEBREWS 13:5 NIV

Unconditional love. We all yearn for it—from our parents, our spouses, our children, our friends. Love *not* based on our performance or accomplishments, but on who we are deep down beneath the fluff. God promises unconditional love to those who honor Him. We don't need to worry about disappointing Him when He gets to know us better—He knows us already. Better than we know ourselves. And He loves us anyway, forever and always.

EVENING
A Word in Due Season

Everyone enjoys a fitting reply;
it is wonderful to say the right thing at the right time!
PROVERBS 15:23 NLT

Ever had a friend approach you at just the right time say, when you were really down and speak something positive and uplifting? Ah, what perfect timing! You needed to hear something good, something pleasant. The right word at the right time was just what the doctor ordered, causing joy to spring up in your soul. The next time you see a friend going through a rough time, decide to speak that "good word."

MORNING
Act in Love

Let all that you do be done in love.
1 CORINTHIANS 16:14 NRSV

Because love is not merely an emotion, it needs to become real
through action. We grow in love as we act in love. Some days the
emotion may overwhelm us; other days we may feel nothing at all.
But if we express our love while making meals, driving the car, talking
to our families, or cleaning the house, God's love will flow through
us to the world around us—and we will see His grace at work.

EVENING
Communication

An open, face-to-face meeting results in peace.
PROVERBS 10:10 MSG

Perhaps growing up you learned that it's more loving to avoid honest
communication than to share what you really feel, think, or need. Maybe
it was easier to blame—or relay messages through someone else rather
than deliver them yourself. Now you notice this approach fails to bring
the results you desire. Sharing directly and honestly while encouraging
others to do the same allows peace to flow into your relationships.
Ask God for help in developing this wise communication skill.

MORNING

Partakers of Joy

*But rejoice inasmuch as you participate in the sufferings of Christ,
so that you may be overjoyed when his glory is revealed.*
1 PETER 4:13 NIV

Ever feel like you've signed on for the suffering but not the joy?
We are called to be partakers in Christ's sufferings. We wouldn't really
know Him if we didn't walk in the valleys occasionally. But, praise God!
We are also partakers in His glorious resurrection. We have the power
of the cross to spur us on! The time has come to trade in those sorrows.
Reach for His unspeakable joy.

EVENING

Young

*Honor and enjoy your Creator
while you're still young.*
ECCLESIASTES 12:1 MSG

Young is a matter of perspective. Some people are old at fifteen,
and others are still young at ninety. As we enjoy the God who
made us, honoring Him in all we do, His grace will keep us young.

MORNING
Keeping Us in Stitches

The secret things belong to the LORD our God.
DEUTERONOMY 29:29 NIV

Have you ever noticed the messy underside of a needlepoint picture? Ugly knots, loose threads, and clashing colors appear random, without pattern. Yet if you turn it over, an exquisite intricate design is revealed, each stitch blending to create a beautiful finished picture. Such is the fabric of our lives. The knots and loose threads may not make sense to us, but the Master Designer has a plan. The secret design *belongs* to Him.

EVENING
Test-a-moany of Praise

Why are you in despair, O my soul? And why have you become disturbed within me? Hope in God, for I shall yet praise him.
PSALM 42:11 NASB

It's said that a testimony is the result of a *test* with a lot of *moaning*. We all endure hardship in this life, and most of us are quick to vocalize our despair. God understands. His own Son cried out "My God, my God, why hast thou forsaken me?" in His darkest moment on the cross. But hope knows there is a victorious day ahead when we will yet praise Him. It's Friday, and Sunday is coming.

Morning
Web of Love

So now I am giving you a new commandment: Love each other.
Just as I have loved you, you should love each other.
JOHN 13:34 NLT

God's grace comes to us through a net of relationships and connections.
Because we know we are totally and unconditionally loved, we can in
turn love others. The connections between us grow ever wider
and stronger, a web of love that unites us all with God.

Evening
Beauty for Ashes

To appoint unto them that mourn in Zion, to give unto them beauty for ashes,
the oil of joy for mourning, the garment of praise for the spirit of heaviness.
ISAIAH 61:3 KJV

Seasons of mourning are difficult to bear, but praise God, He promises
to give us beauty for ashes! He pours joy over us like a scented oil. . .
to woo us out of periods of grieving. Can you feel it washing down on
your head, even now? Can you sense the change in attitude?
Slip on that garment of praise, believer! Shake off the ashes!
Let God's joy overwhelm you!

MORNING

A Deeper Joy

You changed my sorrow into dancing. You took away
my clothes of sadness, and clothed me in happiness.
PSALM 30:11 NCV

Sometimes despair can feel like a deep well. You feel trapped. Can't seem to find your way out to the daylight above. Oh, friend! As deep as your well of sorrow might be, there is a deeper joy. Finding it requires resting your head against the Savior's chest, listening for His heartbeat until it beats in sync with yours. Today, dig deep. . .and find that joy.

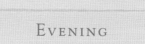

EVENING

Conversation

Watch your words and hold your tongue;
you'll save yourself a lot of grief.
PROVERBS 21:23 MSG

Some of you tend to say almost anything that pops into your mind. This leads to laughter and rollicking conversation. You're the life of the party. Your quieter friends may envy your boldness. Yet sometimes you utter an excited comment and inadvertently hurt someone and cause yourself grief. God doesn't want to change your effervescent personality. He's the one who made you—*and* your more reserved friend. He only wants to temper your thoughts and words to grace others.

MORNING
Large and In Charge

"In this world you will have trouble.
But take heart! I have overcome the world."
JOHN 16:33 NIV

"Who's in charge here?" Most mothers have had the experience of returning home to a chaos-wrecked house. Toys, books, clothes, snack wrappers everywhere. "Why isn't [insert correct answer here: your father, the babysitter, Grandma, etc.] in control?" Our world can sometimes feel chaotic like that. Things appear to be spinning out of control. But we must remember that God is large and in charge. He has a plan.

EVENING
Sense of Timing

But do not forget this one thing, dear friends: With the Lord a
day is like a thousand years, and a thousand years are like a day.
2 PETER 3:8 NIV

God's sense of timing is not the same as ours. What seems like forever to us, an impossible time to wait for something, God sees as exactly the right amount of time, a mere blink of the eye. And on the other hand, God's grace can use a split second to change a person's life.

MORNING
Amazing Love

Your unfailing love, O LORD, is as vast as the heavens;
your faithfulness reaches beyond the clouds.
PSALM 36:5 NLT

God loves you. The Creator of the Universe cares about you, and His love is unconditional and limitless. You can never make Him tired of you; He will never abandon you. You are utterly and completely loved, no matter what, forever and ever. Isn't that amazing?

EVENING
Saints Preserve Us

I will always praise you in the presence of your faithful people.
PSALM 52:9 NIV

We sing, "Lord, I want to be in that number, when the saints go marching in!" But who exactly *are* saints? Exceptionally good people like Saint Nicholas or Mother Teresa? The Bible calls all true believers saints. Some think if their derriere simply graces a pew, they're in. But sitting in church no more makes you a Christian than standing in your closet makes you a vacuum cleaner. Only dedicated Christ-lovers will march into heaven. Are you in that number?

Morning
Count It All Joy!

Consider it pure joy, my brothers and sisters,
whenever you face trials of many kinds.
JAMES 1:2 NIV

Temptations abound. We face them at every turn. On the television.
In our conversations with friends. On the Internet. Today, as you
contemplate the many temptations that life has to offer, count it all
joy! The enemy knows we belong to the King of kings. That's the
only reason he places stumbling blocks in our way. Next time he
rears his ugly head, use joy as a weapon to fight him off.

Evening
The Oil of Joy

Let thy garments be always white;
and let thy head lack no ointment.
ECCLESIASTES 9:8 KJV

What do the words "oil of joy" (Isaiah 61:3) mean to you? Can you
envision the Lord anointing you with that precious oil? Do you feel
it running over your head and down your cheeks? Oh, that we would
always sense the joy of His anointing. That we would see ourselves
as usable to the Kingdom. Today, as you enter your prayer time,
allow the Lord to saturate you with His oil of joy.

MORNING

A Lifetime Award

O Lord, you alone are my hope.
I've trusted you, O LORD, from childhood.
PSALM 71:5 NLT

My heart swelled like an over-inflated balloon. Tears blurred my vision as little Josh bounded for the stage, his blond cowlick flopping in the breeze. As his second-grade Sunday School teacher, I had worked tirelessly to help him memorize ten Bible verses. Josh beamed at the shiny medal encircling his neck, but I knew that his true reward was God's Word implanted in his heart to guide him for the rest of his life.

EVENING

Delight

A good person basks in the delight of GOD.
PROVERBS 12:2 MSG

Don't you love it when a friend says, "It was a delight to be with you"? You feel warm inside just knowing that someone you like likes you back. God likes you, too. *Really.* In fact, He delights in you. You've been made delightful in His sight through Jesus' death and resurrection. You may already know that God *loves* you. After all, that's His nature. But remember, too, that He *likes* you—you are His delight.

MORNING
What You Need

Give me neither poverty nor riches!
Give me just enough to satisfy my needs.
PROVERBS 30:8 NLT

God gives us what we need, and He knows exactly what and how much that is. Whatever He has given you financially, He knows that is what you need right now. Trust His grace. He will satisfy your needs.

EVENING
Adorned with Grace

Don't ever forget kindness and truth. Wear them like a necklace.
PROVERBS 3:3 NCV

Kindness and truth are strands of the same necklace. You should not be so kind that you evade the truth, nor should you be so truthful that you wound others. Instead, adorn yourselves with both strands of this necklace. Wear it with grace.

MORNING

The Spirit Is Willing

"Watch and pray, lest you enter into temptation.
The spirit indeed is willing, but the flesh is weak."
MARK 14:38 NKJV

We've got to be on our guard for unexpected attacks. Temptation can strike at any point. We might feel strong might convince ourselves we're not vulnerable but our flesh is weak! We often end up giving in, even when we're determined not to. Today, ask the Lord to prepare you for any temptations that might come your way. Then, with joy in your heart, be on your guard!

EVENING

Grab and Run

Abraham called the name of that
place The LORD Will Provide.
GENESIS 22:14 NASB

Abraham was asked to do the unthinkable: sacrifice his only son. Can you imagine the terrible struggle he went through in deciding whether to obey God or grab his boy and run? But he chose to exercise his faith and trust that God would provide a way out. And He did. What's *really* in our hearts is revealed during crises. Do we trust God enough to put the lives of our beloved in His hands?

MORNING
Permission to Mourn

When I heard this, I sat down and cried. Then for several days,
I mourned; I went without eating to show my sorrow, and I prayed.
NEHEMIAH 1:4 CEV

Bad news. When it arrives, what's your reaction? Do you scream?
Fall apart? Run away? Nehemiah's response to bad news is a model for
us. First, he vented his sorrow. It's okay to cry and mourn. Christians
suffer pain like everyone else—only, we know the source of inner
healing. Disguising our struggle doesn't make us look more spiritual. . .
just less *real*. Like Nehemiah, our next step is to turn to the only
true source of help and comfort.

EVENING
The Garment of Praise

Awake, awake; put on thy strength, O Zion;
put on thy beautiful garments.
ISAIAH 52:1 KJV

Imagine you've been invited to a grand celebration perhaps a wedding
or a banquet. The clothes in your closet are old. Boring. You need a
new outfit, one worthy of such an occasion. After serious shopping, you
find the perfect dress! It's exquisite and when you wear it, you're in a
party frame of mind. That's what God desires from each of us. . .
to "dress" ourselves in garments of praise. It's time to party!

Morning
Depth of God's Riches

Oh, the depth of the riches of the wisdom and knowledge of God!
How unsearchable his judgments, and his paths beyond tracing out!
ROMANS 11:33 NIV

Money is the way our culture measures value, but we forget that it's just a symbol, a unit of measurement that can never span the infinite value of God's grace. Imagine trying to use a tape measure to stretch across the galaxy, or a teaspoon to determine how much water is in the sea. In the same way, money will always fall short if we use it to try to understand the depth of God's riches.

Evening
Diligence

Look at an ant. Watch it closely; let it teach you. . . . Nobody has to tell it what to do. All summer it stores up food; at harvest it stockpiles provisions.
PROVERBS 6:6–8 MSG

When you see a line of ants traveling across your kitchen counter, it's not really a welcome sight. Yet ants model a few worthwhile lessons about how to accomplish everyday tasks. First, ants self-motivate. They don't need someone to push them or direct their every step. Also, ants do the task at hand without procrastination. They diligently work until they've completed each job. What wise lesson will you take from the ant today?

MORNING
A Joyous Crown

Blessed is the one who perseveres under trial,
because having stood the test, that person will receive the
crown of life that the Lord has promised to those who love him.
JAMES 1:12 NIV

We are so focused on the joys of this life that we sometimes forget
the exquisite joys yet to come in the next. Enduring and overcoming
temptation can bring us great satisfaction here on earth, but imagine
the crown of life we're one day going to receive. Nothing can compare!
Oh, the joy of eternal life. Oh, the thrill of that joyous crown.

EVENING
What's Real

"Then you will experience for yourselves the truth,
and the truth will free you."
JOHN 8:32 MSG

Truth is what is real, while lies are nothing but words. God wants us
to experience what is truly real. Sometimes we would rather hide from
reality, but grace comes to us through truth. No matter how painful
the truth may sometimes seem, it will ultimately set us free.

MORNING

Did You Say Something?

*Call to Me and I will answer you, and I will tell you
great and mighty things, which you do not know.*
JEREMIAH 33:3 NASB

As someone who's been there, done that, you've gotta love the commercial where the husband has his face buried in the newspaper when his wife pops the no-win question: "Does this dress make me look fat?" "You bet," he distractedly replies. God promises to not only hear us when we call to Him, but to answer by teaching us new and amazing things. He's never distracted. He's always listening. And He always cares.

EVENING

If You Build it, He Will Come

*Do not snatch your word of truth from me,
for your regulations are my only hope.*
PSALM 119:43 NLT

Bibles wear and tear. Papers get discarded. Hard drives crash. But memorizing scripture assures us that God's Word will never be lost. His truth will always be at our disposal, any moment of the day or night when we need a word of encouragement, of guidance, of hope. Like a phone call from heaven, our Father communicates to us via scripture implanted in our hearts. But it is up to us to build the signal tower.

MORNING
All You Really Need

Don't wear yourself out trying to get rich;
be wise enough to control yourself.
PROVERBS 23:4 NCV

Some nights we lie awake worrying about bills that need to be paid. When Sunday comes, we sit in church preoccupied with how we can afford to pay for a new car, our kids' college bills, or the taxes. We think about the things we would like to buy. And then we work harder and harder to earn the money we think we have to have. When you catch yourself doing that—stop! God's grace is all you really need.

EVENING
A Joyous Defense

But let all who take refuge in you be glad; let them ever sing for joy.
Spread your protection over them, that those who
love your name may rejoice in you.
PSALM 5:11 NIV

Oh, the pain of betrayal. If you've been hurt by someone you trusted, choose to release that person today. Let it go. God is your defender. He's got your back. Take refuge in Him. And remember, praising Him even in the storm will shift your focus back where it belongs. Praise the Lord! He is our defense!

MORNING

Rooted and Grounded

*"Those on the rocky ground are the ones who receive the word with
joy when they hear it, but they have no root. They believe
for a while, but in the time of testing they fall away."*
LUKE 8:13 NIV

Imagine a sturdy oak tree, one that's been growing for decades.
Its roots run deep. It's grounded. When the storms of life strike,
that tree is going to stand strong. Now think of your own roots.
Do they run deep? When temptations strike, will you stand strong?
Dig into the Word. Receive it with joy. Let it be your foundation.
Plant yourself and let your roots run deep.

EVENING

Direction

*The human mind plans the way,
but the Lord directs the steps.*
PROVERBS 16:9 NRSV

Your carefully thought-through plans may not play out as you
envisioned they would. Life isn't predictable. Certainly it's not perfect.
But one thing is sure. God knows the way through the good *and*
disappointing times. He guides your steps, bringing opportunities across
your path that will shape your character and help you become the wise
woman you long to be. Let God direct you. He knows the way.
He is the absolute best trail guide you could ever have.

Morning
Pay Day

*"Go into all the world and preach
the gospel to all creation."*
MARK 16:15 NASB

One day as our family discussed the Great Commission over dinner,
my salesman husband asked my young daughter if she knew what
commission meant. "Sure," she replied. "It's what you get paid at the
end for what you did in the beginning." Our commission will be paid
in heaven when we're surrounded not only by dear friends and family
with whom we shared our faith, but also the souls reached by missions
we supported with our time, money, and energies.

Evening
True Essence

*"God is spirit, and those who worship
him must worship in spirit and truth."*
JOHN 4:24 NCV

We might be able to fool the flesh-and-blood people around us,
but we cannot deceive the Spirit of God. He sees our truest essence.
The only way to come into His presence is to accept our own truth—
and offer it up to Him. May He give us the grace to truly worship Him!

MORNING
Sharing Life

But if we walk in the light, God himself being the light,
we also experience a shared life with one another.
1 JOHN 1:7 MSG

Some of us are extroverts, and some of us are introverts. But either way, God asks us to share our lives in some way with others. As we walk in His light, He gives us grace to experience a new kind of a life, a life we have in common with the others who share His kingdom.

EVENING
Looming Large

And Isaiah's word: There's the root of our ancestor Jesse,
breaking through the earth and growing tree tall, tall enough
for everyone everywhere to see and take hope!
ROMANS 15:12 MSG

I'll never forget my first view of a giant sequoia on a vacation to the Northwest. Dwarfed by the towering tree, I felt the magnitude of the Ancient of Days. The enormous tree was visible for miles, like a skyscraper against the flat horizon. Isaiah likened Jesus to a tree like that—tall enough for everyone everywhere to see and take hope. And yet some miss Him. She who has eyes to see, let her see!

MORNING
A Thankful Heart

Let the peace of Christ rule in your hearts, since as members
of one body you were called to peace. And be thankful.
COLOSSIANS 3:15 NIV

Have you ever received really great news. . .unexpectedly?
Remember the inexplicable joy that rose up as you received it?
You didn't conjure it up; the joy came quite naturally. Today,
the news is good! God loves you! He cares for your needs and
surrounds you on every side. He is your defense. As you
contemplate these things, watch out! Joy is sure to fill your heart!

EVENING
Hang on to Your Joy!

"The thief comes only to steal and kill and destroy;
I have come that they may have life, and have it to the full."
JOHN 10:10 NIV

Have you ever been the victim of a robbery? It's a terrible feeling,
isn't it? Who would stoop so low? The enemy of your soul is the
ultimate thief. His goal? To steal from you. What is he most interested
in? Your peace of mind. Your joy. He often uses betrayal as a mode of
operation, so be wary! Next time someone hurts you or betrays you
don't let him or her steal your joy. Stand firm!

Morning

It's Not Over

When the wicked die, their hopes die with them,
for they rely on their own feeble strength.
PROVERBS 11:7 NLT

Tony Dungy, Super Bowl champion, coach, and author of *Quiet Strength*, said, "It's because of God's goodness that we can have hope, both for here and the hereafter." Coach Dungy's testimony of eternal hope for those who rely on God's infinite strength touched many hearts after the tragic loss of his teenage son. Death is not the end. There is a hope, a future for those who choose to *not* rely on their own feeble strength.

Evening

Encouragement

The words of the godly encourage many.
PROVERBS 10:21 NLT

Everyone needs encouragement. Your best friend needs it. Your son and daughter need it. Your pastor needs it. So does your sister. Your boss needs it. The deliveryman needs it. If you're married, your spouse needs it—even though he may not act like he does. And what about you? Do you crave some encouragement today? It's okay to verbalize your desire, just as it's good to encourage others with your words. Mutual encouragement makes the world a richer place.

MORNING
Loving Support

*Let us think of ways to motivate one
another to acts of love and good works.*
HEBREWS 10:24 NLT

Imagine that you're sitting in the bleachers watching one of your favorite young people play a sport. You jump up and cheer for him. You make sure he knows you're there, shouting out encouragement. Hearing your voice, he jumps higher, runs faster. That is the sort of excitement and support we need to show others around us. When we do all we can to encourage each other, love and good deeds will burst from us all.

EVENING
On Truth's Side

*We're rooting for the truth to win out in you.
We couldn't possibly do otherwise.*
2 CORINTHIANS 13:8 MSG

As we look at the world around us, we can see that people often prefer falsehoods to truth. They choose to live in a world that soothes their anxiety, rather than face life's reality. We cannot force people to acknowledge what they don't want to face, but we can do all we can to encourage them and build them up. We can cheer for the truth, trusting that God's grace is always on truth's side.

Morning

Hem Your Blessings

Everything God created is good,
and to be received with thanks.
1 Timothy 4:4 msg

Sometimes we walk through seasons of blessing and forget to be grateful. It's easy, with the busyness of life, to overlook the fact that Someone has made provision to cover the monthly bills. Someone has graced us with good health. Someone has given us friends and loved ones to share our joys and sorrows. Today, pause a moment and thank the Lord for the many gifts He's poured out. Hem in those blessings!

Evening

Prince on a White Steed

I promise that from that day on, you will
call me your husband instead of your master.
Hosea 2:16 cev

I have two husbands. If you're a Christ-lover and married, you do, too. The Bible considers believers "the bride of Christ" and draws many parallels to a marital relationship (Ephesians 5:25). Christ provides for and protects His people. And even better than many flawed human marriages, He loves us unconditionally and refuses to divorce us no matter what. He's our prince on a white steed. . .forever.

MORNING
Streets of Treats

What you hope for is kept safe for you in heaven.
COLOSSIANS 1:5 CEV

Heaven. Will the streets really be paved with gold? Or even better—chocolate? (Have you noticed it's impossible to keep a stash of chocolate safely hidden? Kids can sniff out that stuff like bloodhounds.) No, if our earthly treasures are our source of security and hope, we're in trouble. Rust, thieves, decay, recession. . .*things* just aren't safe. But peace? Joy? Reveling forever in our Lord's presence? All waiting for us safely in heaven. (But who says we can't hope for Godiva-cobbled streets?)

EVENING
Come on. . .Get Happy!

But even if you should suffer for what is right, you are blessed.
"Do not fear their threats; do not be frightened."
1 PETER 3:14 NIV

It's one thing to suffer because of something you've done wrong; it's another to suffer for doing right. Even when we're unjustly persecuted, God wants us to respond in the right way. If you're suffering as a result of something you've done for the Lord. . .be happy! Keep a stiff upper lip! This, too, shall pass, and you *can* come through it with a joyful attitude.

MORNING
Christ Followers

*"This is what the LORD All-Powerful says:
'Do what is right and true. Be kind and merciful to each other.'"*
ZECHARIAH 7:9 NCV

As Christ's followers, we need to interact with others the way
He did when He was on earth. That means we don't lie to each
other, and we don't use others. Instead, we practice kindness
and mercy. We let God's grace speak through our mouths.

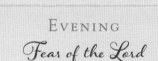

EVENING
Fear of the Lord

The fear of the LORD is the beginning of wisdom.
PROVERBS 9:10 NRSV

Fear blocks intimacy. It can hinder you from trying new things and
cause you to obsess about finances or health. Fear threatens your
contentment—even when you don't want it to. You want to be wise;
free from fear. Then you read: "The fear of the Lord is the beginning
of wisdom." *Must I fear God, too?* Yet, to "fear" God means to respect
and reverence Him with deepest adoration. When you do,
everyday fear begins to fade and wisdom flourishes.

MORNING

Thanks. . .Again!

*How can we thank God enough for you in return for all
the joy we have in the presence of our God because of you?*

1 THESSALONIANS 3:9 NIV

Think of the people God has placed in your life—your family members, friends, coworkers, and other loved ones. They bring such joy and happiness to your life, don't they? Now contemplate this. . .what if you'd never met any of them? How different would your life be? These folks are such a gift! God has given them to you as a special present. . .one you need to remember to thank Him for.

EVENING

Growing in Grace

*This is my prayer for you: that your love will grow more and more;
that you will have knowledge and understanding with your love.*

PHILIPPIANS 1:9 NCV

God wants us to be spiritually mature. He wants us to love more deeply, and at the same time, He wants us to reach deeper into wisdom and understanding. This is not something we can accomplish in our own strength with our own abilities. Only God can make us grow in grace.

MORNING
Soul Sister

"I always see the Lord near me, and I will not be afraid with him at my right side. Because of this, my heart will be glad, my words will be joyful, and I will live in hope."
ACTS 2:25–26 CEV

Laughter is the soul sister of joy; they often travel together. Humor is the primary catalyst for releasing joy into our souls and making our hearts glad. It's healthy for us, too! Laughter is cleansing and healing, a powerful salve for the wounds of life. . .a natural medicine and tremendous stress reliever. Laughing is to joy what a 50% OFF sign is to shopping. It motivates us to seek more, more, more!

EVENING
Blameless

[Jesus] has brought you into his own presence, and you are holy and blameless as you stand before him without a single fault.
COLOSSIANS 1:22 NLT

Holiness. Wouldn't we all like to attain it? But it's impossible. Even if we shave our heads, eat only birdseed, forsake makeup, and wear nothing but mumus, we still wouldn't be holy. We'd just be ugly. The only way we can achieve holiness is through Jesus, who by His death on our behalf ushers us into the presence of God, blameless, beautiful, and whole. And we can leave our mumus at home.

MORNING

Overflowing Love

*And may the Lord make your love for one another and for all
people grow and overflow, just as our love for you overflows.*
1 THESSALONIANS 3:12 NLT

As a very young child, you thought you were the center of the world.
As you grew older, you had to go through the painful process of
learning that others' feelings were as important as yours. God's grace
wants to lift your perspective even higher, though. He wants
you to overflow with love for other people.

EVENING

A Joyous Treasure

*"The kingdom of heaven is like treasure hidden in a field.
When a man found it, he hid it again, and then in his
joy went and sold all he had and bought that field."*
MATTHEW 13:44 NIV

Have you ever stumbled across a rare treasure—one so priceless
that you would be willing to trade everything you own to have it?
If you've given your heart to Christ, if you've accepted His work
on Calvary, then you have already obtained the greatest treasure
of all. . .new life in Him. Oh, what immeasurable joy comes from
knowing He's placed that treasure in your heart for all eternity!

MORNING

Thanks Be to God!

*I am grateful that God always makes it
possible for Christ to lead us to victory.*
2 CORINTHIANS 2:14 CEV

God has created us to be victors, not victims. We are image-bearers
of Christ and born to triumph! So, how do you see yourself today?
Have you made up your mind to overcome in the areas where you've
struggled? One way to assure your victory is to praise God for it. . .
even before it happens. That's right! Praise your way through!
Oh, the joy of triumphing in Christ!

EVENING

Generosity

*A quietly given gift soothes an irritable person;
a heartfelt present cools a hot temper.*
PROVERBS 21:14 MSG

A knee-jerk reaction to an irritable clerk is to snap back. When a
friend shoots an angry remark your direction, you may want to
retaliate. However, when you offer the gift of a quiet response or
understanding word, your generous act can diffuse the tension. Even a
gift of time or money can make a positive difference. Offer homemade
cookies, lunch out, to take out the trash, or help with another project.
Your quietly given gift can cool a heated situation.

MORNING
Smiling Hearts

Weeping may last for the night,
but a shout of joy comes in the morning.
PSALM 30:5 NASB

What woman hasn't seen the dim underbelly of 2 a.m. through hot tears? God gave us emotionally sensitive spirits and is willing to sit with us as we weep through the long, hard night. Sometimes "night" lasts for a season. But He promises that the sun will eventually rise. And on that glorious morning, we'll be filled with so much joy, even our hearts will smile. Joy is appreciated most in the wake of disappointment.

EVENING
The Missing Pieces

Trust the LORD with all your heart,
and don't depend on your own understanding.
PROVERBS 3:5 NCV

Life is confusing. No matter how hard we try, we can't always make sense of it. We don't like it when that happens, and so we keep trying to determine what's going on, as though we were trying puzzle piece after puzzle piece to fill in a picture we long to see. Sometimes though, we have to accept that in this life we will never be able to see the entire image. We have to trust God's grace for the missing pieces.

MORNING
Healed Past

*"All their past sins will be forgotten, and they will
live because of the righteous things they have done."*
EZEKIEL 18:22 NLT

We have the feeling that we can't do anything about the past. We
think all our mistakes are back there behind us, carved in stone. But
God's creative power is amazing, and His grace can heal even the past.
Yesterday's sins are pulled out like weeds, while the good things we have
done are watered so that they grow and flourish into the present. Give
your past to God. His grace is big enough to bring healing even to your
worst memories.

EVENING
Whole and Healed

*Pray for each other so that you can live together whole and healed. The prayer
of a person living right with God is something powerful to be reckoned with.*
JAMES 5:16 MSG

Do you have soul siblings? Brothers and sisters in Christ? Caring people
who pray *for* you and *with* you about, well, everything? Like a life
preserver in a turbulent sea, prayer partners are buoyancy for the
soul and security through any storm. Heart-bonds, once established,
create a trusting environment where we can bare our souls before
the Lord in mutual prayer to become whole and healed.
Prayer partners are warm hugs from God.

MORNING
A Royal Vision

Yes, joyful are those who live like this!
Joyful indeed are those whose God is the LORD.
PSALM 144:15 NLT

How wonderful to realize you're God's child. He loves you and wants nothing but good for you. Doesn't knowing you're His daughter send waves of joy through your soul? How happy we are when we recognize that we are princesses. . .children of the most high God! Listen closely as He whispers royal secrets in your ear. Your heavenly Father offers you keys to the Kingdom. . .and vision for the road ahead.

EVENING
A Joyful Noise

Make a joyful noise unto the LORD, all ye lands.
PSALM 100:1 KJV

How do we praise God for His many blessings? If we follow the pattern of Old Testament saints, then we lift our voices in thanksgiving! We let others know. With a resounding voice, we echo our praises, giving thanks for all He has done, and all He continues to do. So, praise Him today! Make a joyful noise!

MORNING
JOY: Jesus Occupying You

May all who fear you find in me a cause for joy,
for I have put my hope in your word.
PSALM 119:74 NLT

Have you ever met someone you immediately knew was filled with joy?
The kind of effervescent joy that bubbles up and overflows,
covering everyone around her with warmth and love and acceptance.
We love to be near people filled with Jesus-joy. And even more,
as Christians we want to be *like* them!

EVENING
Gratitude

Ears to hear and eyes to see—
both are gifts from the LORD.
PROVERBS 20:12 NLT

Everything you have is a gift from God. The air you breathe,
the sunset you enjoy, the rain that nourishes your garden, your work,
love of family and friends, your taste buds, freedom, music, a bird's song,
art, the creativity to design. All things are God's, and He shares them
with you. *To bring you pleasure.* What are you grateful for today?
Pause for a moment and thank Him for all His gifts.

MORNING
Looking Forward

*I focus on this one thing: Forgetting the past
and looking forward to what lies ahead.*
PHILIPPIANS 3:13 NLT

As followers of Christ, we are people who look forward rather than
backward. We have all made mistakes, but God does not want us to
dwell on them, wallowing in guilt and discouragement. Instead, He calls
us to let go of the past, trusting Him to deal with it. His grace is new
every moment.

EVENING
Most Important

*Tune your ears to the world of Wisdom;
set your heart on a life of Understanding.*
PROVERBS 2:3 MSG

What do you listen to most? Do you hear the world's voice, telling
you to buy, buy, buy; to dress and look a certain way; to focus on things
that won't last? Or have you tuned your ears to hear the quiet voice of
God's wisdom? You can tell the answer to that question by your response
to yet another question: What is most important to you? Things?
Or the intangible grace of true understanding?

MORNING
"Happy Is He..." (or She!)

Where there is no vision, the people perish:
but he that keepeth the law, happy is he.
PROVERBS 29:18 KJV

Ever wish you could see into tomorrow? Wish you knew what was coming around the bend? While we can't see into the future, we can prepare for it, by trusting God to bring us His very best. And while our "literal" vision can't glimpse the unseen tomorrow, we can prepare for it by staying close to the Lord and spending time in His Word. Peace and joy come when we trust God with our future!

EVENING
Mosaic Masterpieces

God gives us what it takes to do all that we do.
2 CORINTHIANS 3:5 CEV

As an orthopedic occupational therapist, I work with broken people. Lives are forever altered by strokes, accidents, disease. "I can't live like this" is a phrase often uttered at the beginning of the rehabilitation journey. But we don't know just how many ways we *can* live until we depend on God to give us what we need. Not only to live, but live productive, fulfilling lives. He creates mosaic masterpieces from the pieces of our lives.

MORNING
Justice for All?

Our God, you save us, and your fearsome deeds answer our
prayers for justice! You give hope to people everywhere on earth.
PSALM 65:5 CEV

It's not fair! How many times have we uttered this indignant cry when life handed us injustice? Our work goes unrecognized; our best efforts are rejected; calamity seems to roost on our doorstep. We demand justice— it's what we deserve, right? But what about all those times we've misstepped or misjudged? James 2:13 tells us that *mercy* triumphs over justice. Mercy forgives mistakes and *doesn't* dole out what is deserved. Mercy—like a jail sentence pardoned. Mercy—like a man on a cross.

EVENING
Abounding with Blessings

A faithful man shall abound with blessings.
PROVERBS 28:20 KJV

To *abound* means to have more than enough. When you're abounding, all of your needs are met. . .and then some! How wonderful to go through such seasons. So, what do we have to do to qualify for these "more than enough" blessings? Only one thing. Be found faithful. Trust God during the lean seasons. Don't give up! Then, when the "abounding" seasons come, you can truly rejoice!

MORNING

Renewal

"Look, the winter is past,
and the rains are over and gone."
SONG OF SOLOMON 2:11 NLT

Dreary times of cold and rain come to us all. Just as the earth needs those times to renew itself, so do we. As painful as those times are, grace works through them to make us into the people God has called us to be. But once those times are over, there's no need to continue to dwell on them. Go outside and enjoy the sunshine!

EVENING

Honesty

The LORD wants honest balances and scales.
PROVERBS 16:11 NCV

God values truth-telling. Years ago people used stone weights on scales to determine the measurements of the products they sold. Dishonest store owners labeled the stones incorrectly to pad their profits. Dishonesty saddened God then as it does now. God loves for his children to be honest. Yet, sometimes it seems more comfortable to avoid the truth if it isn't to your advantage. Being honest with your personal and professional dealings and relationships takes God-given courage—*and* it's incredibly freeing.

MORNING
A Joyous Stand

May he give you the desire of your heart and make all your plans succeed.
We will shout for joy when you are victorious and will lift
up our banners in the name of our God.
PSALM 20:4–5 NIV

It's hard to have a vision for tomorrow if you're not excited about today!
Each day is a gift, after all, and an opportunity to live for Christ.
Today, take a stand for the things you believe in. Lift high His Name.
Not only will you bring joy to His heart (and your own), you will
find yourself looking forward to a joy-filled tomorrow.

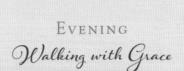

EVENING
Walking with Grace

"Give me an understanding heart so that I can govern your
people well and know the difference between right and wrong."
1 KINGS 3:9 NLT

We are not kings who rule nations, but all of us have spheres of influence
and authority, whether at home or at work. As Christ's followers, we
must be careful not to abuse our authority. Instead, we should seek to
understand, to walk with grace the straight path of kindness and wisdom.

MORNING
As the Tide Turns

He will not falter or be discouraged till he establishes justice on earth.
In his law the islands will put their hope.
ISAIAH 42:4 NIV

Change. . .besides our unalterable Lord, it's the only thing constant in this world. Yet the only person who likes change is a baby with a wet diaper. Isaiah prophesied that the Almighty will one day create positive change on earth. Like the tides that clean beach debris after a storm, positive change washes away the old and refreshes with the new. In this we hope.

EVENING
Slathered in SPF

You are my refuge and my shield;
I have put my hope in your word.
PSALM 119:114 NIV

These days, the word *shield* evokes images of glistening sunbathers dotting beaches and carefree children slathered in sunscreen. Like the psalmist's metal shield, sunscreen deflects dangerous rays, preventing them from penetrating vulnerable skin—higher SPF for more protection. When we are immersed in God's Word, we erect a shield that deflects Satan's attempts to penetrate our weak flesh. Internalizing more of God's Word creates a higher SPF: Scripture Protection Factor. Are you well-coated?

MORNING
You Will Live

Their past sins will be forgiven, and they will live.
EZEKIEL 33:16 CEV

Do you ever feel doomed? Do you feel as though your mistakes are
waiting to fall on your head, like a huge rock that will crush the life
out of you? We all have moments like that. But God's grace doesn't
let that enormous boulder drop. His forgiveness catches it
and rolls it away. You will live after all!

EVENING
Joyous Members

Just as a body, though one, has many parts,
but all its many parts form one body,
so it is with Christ.
1 CORINTHIANS 12:12 NIV

It's fun to look around the church on any given Sunday morning and
see the various gifts at work. One teaches, the other leads worship.
One edifies, another handles the finances. God didn't make us all alike.
Praise Him for that! He recognizes our differences. How do we merge
all of those unique people into one body? We don't! That's God's job.
We simply do our best to remain unified members of a joyous family.

MORNING
An Ear to Hear

He that hath an ear, let him hear
what the Spirit saith unto the churches.
REVELATION 2:17 KJV

We need to "lean in" to the Lord on a daily basis. Listen to His still, small voice. Catch a glimpse of His vision for the church. Ride on the wind of the Spirit. Today, as you draw close to the Lord, listen closely. What is He speaking into your life? May your joy be full as you "tune in" to the voice of the Holy Spirit.

EVENING
Humility

Don't assume that you know it all. Run to God! . . .
Your body will glow with health, your very bones will vibrate with life!
PROVERBS 3:7–8 MSG

It's unrealistic to think you can figure out everything and everyone— even though you're a capable woman and some say you have eyes in the back of your head! Seriously, it's just too much pressure to try to know it *all* month after month, year after year. The stress takes a toll on your health. So as a woman committed to making wise choices, you can release your need to know, turn your concerns over to God, and relax.

MORNING
Up Is the Only Out

Let them lie face down in the dust, for there may be hope at last.
LAMENTATIONS 3:29 NLT

The Old Testament custom for grieving people was to lie prostrate and cover themselves with ashes. Perhaps the thought was that when you're wallowing in the dust, at least you can't descend any further. There's an element of hope in knowing that, from there, there's only one way to go: up. If a recent loss has you sprawled in the dust, know that God doesn't waste pain in our lives. He will use it for some redeeming purpose.

EVENING
First Priorities

For Wisdom is better than all the trappings of wealth;
nothing you could wish for holds a candle to her.
PROVERBS 8:11 MSG

What do you value most? You may know the answer you are "supposed" to give to that question, but you can tell the real answer by where your time and energy are focused. Do you spend most of your time working for and thinking about money and physical wealth, or do you make wisdom and grace your first priorities?

MORNING
Valuable

Better to be patient than powerful;
better to have self-control than to conquer a city.
PROVERBS 16:32 NLT

Our world values visible power. We appreciate things like prestige and skill, wealth and influence. But God looks at things differently. From His perspective, the quiet, easily overlooked quality of patience is far more valuable than any worldly power. Patience makes room for others' needs and brokenness. Patience creates a space in our lives for God's grace to flow through us.

EVENING
Double Scoop

Know also that wisdom is like honey for you:
If you find it, there is a future hope for you.
PROVERBS 24:14 NIV

Chocolate chunk cookies. Sock-it-to-me pound cake. Ice cream sundaes with cherries on top. Sweets add zest to the mundane, don't they? (Not to mention cellulite to the thighs!) In the same way, wisdom enhances our souls. What kind of wisdom? Not mathematical equations, science facts, or Latin verbs. No, the wisdom embedded in God's Word is what sweetens our spirits and adds zing to our mundane lives. How about a double scoop today?

MORNING
Seeing the Invisible

*Now faith is confidence in what we hope
for and assurance about what we do not see.*
HEBREWS 11:1 NIV

You must look at your future as hopeful, and filled with wonderful
"what ifs." No, you're not promised tomorrow. But if you give up on
your hopes and dreams, if you lose sight of the plans the Lord has laid
on your heart, they will surely not come to pass. Trust God to make the
invisible. . .visible. And in the meantime, rejoice! You have a lot to
look forward to!

EVENING
A New Season

*"A woman giving birth to a child has pain because her time has come;
but when her baby is born she forgets the anguish because
of her joy that a child is born into the world."*
JOHN 16:21 NIV

If you've ever delivered a child, you know the pain associated with
childbirth. But that's not what you remember after the fact, is it?
No, as you hold that little one in your arms, only one thing remains. . .
the supernatural joy you experience as you gaze into your newborn's
eyes. The same is true with the seasons we walk through. Sorrows
will end, and joy will rise to the surface once again!

MORNING
Welcome Back

Train up a child in the way he should go;
and when he is old, he will not depart from it.
PROVERBS 22:6 KJV

I'll never forget the tender bedtime family gatherings on my sister's bed when I was a child. After reading a Bible story from the big picture Bible, we took turns praying. When I had children, I established the same tradition in our home. The Bible promises that if we instill God's Word and principles in our children, they will one day return to it. It may take time, but God's Word will *not* return void.

EVENING
Integrity

God. . .relishes integrity.
PROVERBS 11:20 MSG

God cares about integrity. He wants you to be the same inside as you appear outside. Some may think this integrity dilemma only shows up when someone pretends to love God but really doesn't. But there's a painful flip side that women encounter when they deeply desire God but live to please someone else instead. Luckily, there's a cure. Courageously permit your heart to influence your actions, even when it's uncomfortable. God will help.

MORNING
Quiet Time

Be still before the LORD, and wait patiently for him.
PSALM 37:7 NRSV

Our lives are busy. Responsibilities crowd our days, and at night as we go to bed, our minds often continue to be preoccupied with the day's work, ticking off a mental to-do list even as we fall asleep. We need to set aside time to quiet our hearts. In those moments, we can let go of all our to-dos and wait for God's grace to take action in our lives.

EVENING
Grace Multiplied

*Honor the LORD with your wealth and with
the best part of everything you produce.*
PROVERBS 3:9 NLT

We connect the word *wealth* with money, but long ago the word meant "happiness, prosperity, well-being." If you think about your wealth in this light, then the word encompasses far more of your life. Your health, your abilities, your friends, your family, your physical strength, and your creative energy—all of these are parts of your true wealth. Grace brought all of these riches into your life, and when we use them to honor God, grace is multiplied still more.

MORNING
The Key to Happiness

He who heeds the word wisely will find good,
and whoever trusts in the LORD, happy is he.
PROVERBS 16:20 NKJV

Want the key to true happiness? Try wisdom. When others around you are losing their heads, losing their cool, and losing sleep over their decisions, choose to react differently. Step up to the plate. Handle matters wisely. Wise choices always lead to joyous outcomes. And along the way, you will be setting an example for others around you to follow. So, c'mon. . .get happy! Get wisdom!

EVENING
Choosing Last

Do you see a man wise in his own eyes?
There is more hope for a fool than for him.
PROVERBS 26:12 NASB

When my first national article was published, I proudly stood in the middle of a bookstore, held the magazine aloft, and announced that this was *my* article and *my* picture. One kind elderly lady smiled but everyone else simply ignored me. It was a painful lesson in humility. Humility is a learned skill, not an inborn trait. That's why Jesus taught about *choosing* the mind-set of humility. The last shall be first.

MORNING
Who's Your Daddy?

His name is the LORD. A father to the fatherless.
PSALM 68:4–5 NIV

His father left when my friend Ben was two. Ben recognized him once—from pictures—at a family funeral, but his father intentionally turned away. When Ben was thirty-five, with a family of his own, his father suddenly showed up, seeking a relationship. Sadly, he was diagnosed with cancer shortly after their reunion and died of cancer within one year. Ben mourned but knew his real paternal relationship was with God, the Father to the fatherless.

EVENING
The Joy Set before Me

Fixing our eyes on Jesus, the pioneer and perfecter of faith.
For the joy set before him endured the cross, scorning its shame,
and sat down at the right hand of the throne of God.
HEBREWS 12:2 NIV

Jesus walked through many seasons in His ministry here on earth. He walked through seasons of great favor, when crowds flocked to Him and when voices cried out, "Blessed is He who comes in the name of the Lord!" But He also walked through seasons of ultimate rejection as He headed up Golgotha's hill. We will go through good times and bad, but like Jesus, we can say, "But for the joy set before me. . .I will endure."

MORNING
Quiet Grace

Patient persistence pierces through indifference;
gentle speech breaks down rigid defenses.
PROVERBS 25:15 MSG

When we're in the midst of an argument, we often become fixated on winning. We turn conflicts into power struggles, and we want to come out the victor. By sheer force, if necessary, we want to shape people to our will. But that is not the way God treats us. His grace is gentle and patient rather than loud and forceful. We need to follow His example and let His quiet grace speak through us in His timing rather than ours.

EVENING
Intentionality

She looks over a field and buys it, then,
with money she's put aside, plants a garden.
PROVERBS 31:16 MSG

You've heard it before: *be proactive.* But what does it mean? In part it means to *initiate* wise change instead of merely reacting to problems. For example, you set a goal to eat healthier. You pray about it, make a plan, research options, and visualize the outcome. But that's not enough. You need to *act* on your plan to see it come to fruition. You and your goals are important to God. Ask Him to help you act intentionally.

MORNING
Seek Out Wisdom

*I applied mine heart to know,
and to search, and to seek out wisdom.*
ECCLESIASTES 7:25 KJV

Remember when you participated in your first Easter egg hunt?
You searched under every bush, every tree until you found one of
those shiny eggs. The quest for wisdom is much like that. You've got
to look under a lot of shrubs to find it, especially in this day and age.
Oh, but what a prize! Today, as you apply your heart to the Word
of God, seek out wisdom. What a joyous treasure!

EVENING
Never Bought

*They trust in their riches and brag about all of their wealth.
You cannot buy back your life or pay off God!*
PSALM 49:6–7 CEV

We humans are easily confused about what real wealth is.
We think that money can make us strong. We assume that physical
possessions will enhance our importance and dignity in others' eyes.
But life is not for sale. And grace can never be bought.

MORNING
Live and Learn

Lead me by your truth and teach me, for you are the
God who saves me. All day long I put my hope in you.
PSALM 25:5 NLT

Acquiring spiritual wisdom is a fluid process. Trickles pool into mighty
reservoirs from which we draw hope. God is right beside us moment by
moment, day by day, guiding us, teaching us, feeding our reservoirs. But
if we freeze the Holy Spirit out of our lives by apathetic or indifferent
attitudes, the trickle solidifies into ice and the flow of wisdom is
blocked. If we keep our minds open to God's everyday lessons, just
watch the river surge!

EVENING
The Foundation and Finale

I hope to see you soon, and then we will
talk face to face. Peace be with you.
3 JOHN 1:14–15 NLT

My prayer is that the message you receive from this book is that Christ
is the ultimate source of hope. We can live without many things, but
we cannot live without hope. It's the air we breathe, the water that
invigorates every molecule of our being, the motivation that drives us.
Hope enriches and empowers us, connecting us with our Papa God.
Hope is the essence of our faith. It's the foundation and the finale.

Morning
Another Moment Longer

Wait patiently for the LORD. Be brave and courageous.
Yes, wait patiently for the LORD.
PSALM 27:14 NLT

Patience is all about waiting things out. It's about holding on another moment longer. It means enduring hard times. As a younger person, you probably felt you couldn't possibly endure certain things, but the older you get, the more you realize that you can. If you just wait long enough, the tide always turns. Hold on. Your life will change. God's grace will rescue you.

Evening
Change Is around the Bend . . .

"'I will make them and the places surrounding my hill a blessing.
I will send down showers in season; there will be showers of blessing.'"
EZEKIEL 34:26 NIV

How do we shift from one project to the next? One phase of life to the next? We can move forward with joy leading the way when we realize that God is the Giver of the seasons. He designed them and showers us with blessings as we move through each one, even the tough ones! Good news! Change is always just around the bend. Oh, the joy of knowing the hard times won't last.

MORNING
The Words of My Mouth

She speaks with wisdom, and faithful instruction is on her tongue.
PROVERBS 31:26 NIV

Have you ever known someone who epitomized wisdom? What set her apart from others of your acquaintance? A truly wise person thinks carefully before speaking and only opens her mouth when wisdom is ready to flow out. Kindness is on her tongue. There's great joy in "becoming" wise in this way. Today, guard your tongue! Think before you speak. By doing so, you bring joy to others. . .and yourself.

EVENING
Kindness

What is desired. . .is kindness.
PROVERBS 19:22 NKJV

Have you noticed that kindness sometimes seems like a lost commodity? It's understandable. Everyone's in such a hurry and on alert 24/7. You hear recorded messages when you call for an important appointment. When you need help on the highway, it's often "tough luck." Then someone graces you with a spontaneous act of kindness and your mood brightens. God knew that would happen. It's His plan. He treats you with loving-kindness, so you can share it with others.

MORNING
Getting to Know You

*For the law never made anything perfect. But now we have confidence
in a better hope, through which we draw near to God.*

HEBREWS 7:19 NLT

Following Old Testament law used to be considered the way to achieve
righteousness, but obeying rules just doesn't work for fallible humans.
We mess up. We fail miserably. Then Jesus came and provided a better
way to draw near to God. He bridged the gap by offering us a personal
relationship rather than rules. Together we laugh, cry, love, grieve,
rejoice. We get to *know* our Papa God through our personal relationship
with Him.

EVENING
Riches That Last

*"Yes, a person is a fool to store up earthly
wealth but not have a rich relationship with God."*

LUKE 12:21 NLT

Why would we want money in the bank and a house full
of stuff if we lived in a world that was empty of grace?
Only in God do we find the riches that will last forever.

Morning
Peaceful Hearts

You will keep in perfect peace all who trust in you,
all whose thoughts are fixed on you!
ISAIAH 26:3 NLT

Peace seems very far away sometimes. But it's not! Peace isn't an emotion we can work up in our own strength. It's one of the gifts of grace God longs to give us. All we need to do is focus on Him. As we give Him all our worries, one by one, every day, He will do His part: He will keep our hearts at peace.

Evening
Shouts of Joy

He will yet fill your mouth with laughter
and your lips with shouts of joy.
JOB 8:21 NIV

Do you remember the last time you laughed till you cried? For many of us, it's been far too long. Stress tends to steal our joy, leaving us humorless and oh-so-serious. But lightness and fun haven't disappeared forever. They may be buried beneath the snow of a long, wintery life season, but spring is coming, girls. Laughter will bloom again, and our hearts will soar as our lips shout with joy. Grasp that hope!

MORNING
A Net of Love

No one has ever seen God; but if we love one another,
God lives in us and his love is made complete in us.
1 JOHN 4:12 NIV

It's hard to be a good witness if you've got a sour expression on your face. People aren't usually won to the Lord by grumpy friends and coworkers. If you hope to persuade people that life in Jesus is the ultimate, then you've got to let your enthusiasm shine through. Before you reach for the net, spend some time on your knees, asking for an infusion of joy. Then, go catch some fish!

EVENING
Lift Up Your Voice!

And at midnight Paul and Silas prayed, and sang praises unto God:
and the prisoners heard them.
ACTS 16:25 KJV

Are you a closet praiser? Happy to worship God in the privacy of your own home but nervous about opening up and praising Him in public? Oh, may this be the day you break through that barrier. Corporate praise coming together with your brothers and sisters in the Lord to worship Him is powerful! May you come to know the fullness of His joy as you worship side by side with fellow believers!

MORNING
Fresh and Green

They will still bear fruit in old age,
they will stay fresh and green.
PSALM 92:14 NIV

Doris, a tiny eighty-nine-year-old widow in my Bible study, is teaching me how to be a blessing. That's her prayer every morning of her life: *Lord, make me a blessing to someone today.* And sure enough, God uses her to touch lives in His name—helping a frantic woman find her lost keys; taking a sick neighbor to the doctor; offering a friendly word to the grumpy, wheelchair-bound man. Little blessings are big indeed to those in need.

EVENING
Leadership

Good leadership is a channel of water controlled by GOD;
he directs it to whatever ends he chooses.
PROVERBS 21:1 MSG

You are a leader. Maybe you don't think so, but you are. Someone looks up to you and would like your support, advice, and encouragement. Perhaps you doubt your ability to lead well. Still, you long to live and inspire others with a sincere heart—with intentionality, wisdom, and grace. Be encouraged, because God loves to guide you. Partner with Him and be assured that He's working in you to influence others for good.

Morning
Peace Rules

And let the peace that comes from Christ rule in your hearts.
For as members of one body you are called to live in peace.
COLOSSIANS 3:15 NLT

Peace is a way of living our lives. It happens when we let Christ's peace
into our lives to rule over our emotions, our doubts, and our worries,
and then go one step more and let His peace control the way we live.
Peace is God's gift of grace to us, but it is also the way to a graceful life,
the path to harmony with the world around us.

Evening
Wise Enough to Lead

"To God belong wisdom and power;
counsel and understanding are his."
JOB 12:13 NIV

The word *wisdom* comes from the same root words that have to
do with vision, the ability to see into a deeper spiritual reality.
Where else can we turn for the grace to see beneath life's surface
except to God? Who else can we trust to be strong enough
and wise enough to lead us to our eternal home?

MORNING

Blooming for All to See

Since God chose you to be the holy people he loves,
you must clothe yourselves with tenderhearted mercy,
kindness, humility, gentleness, and patience.
COLOSSIANS 3:12 NLT

Have you ever noticed that we're naturally drawn to people who are fun to be around. . .people who radiate joy? They are like a garden of thornless roses: they put off a beautiful aroma and draw people quite naturally. If you want to win people to the Lord, then woo them with your kindness. Put off an inviting aroma. Win them with your love. Radiate joy!

EVENING

Designer Label

We wish that each of you would always be eager to
show how strong and lasting your hope really is.
HEBREWS 6:11 CEV

Our behavior is always on display and, like it or not, we are judged by our actions. . .and inactions. Without an explanation for our behavior—that we're motivated by faith to be Christlike—people will make up their own ideas: *Her mama taught her right; she was just born nice; she acts sweet so everyone will like her.* Isn't it better to be up-front and give credit to the One we're emulating? Wear the label of your Designer proudly.

MORNING
Rocky Road

*Through the Spirit we eagerly await by
faith the righteousness for which we hope.*
GALATIANS 5:5 NIV

My daughter's five-pound Russian Terror (oops—that's Terrier) is
anything but righteous. Rocky dashes after cars, nibbles poisonous
plants, and routinely ingests ripped-apart rugs. In order to guide said
pup along the path of righteousness, doors must close. The only opened
doors invite him to destinations specially prepared for him.
Our paths of righteousness are also guided by the One who shuts doors
according to what's best for us. So, girlfriends—enough howling,
whining, and scratching at closed doors!

EVENING
Joy. . .a Powerful Force

*Praise ye the LORD. Praise God in his sanctuary:
praise him in the firmament of his power.*
PSALM 150:1 KJV

There's just something amazing about being in a powerful worship
service when all of God's children are like-minded, lifting up their
voices in joyful chorus. The next time you're in such a service,
pause a moment and listen. . .really listen. Can you sense the joy
that sweeps across the room? The wonder? Oh, what a powerful
force we are when we praise in one accord!

Morning
An All-the-Time Thing!

Pray diligently. Stay alert, with your eyes wide open in gratitude.
COLOSSIANS 4:2 MSG

Prayer is not a sometimes thing. It's an all-the-time thing! We need to pray every day, being careful to keep the lines of communication open between God and ourselves all through the day, moment by moment. When we make prayer a habit, we won't miss the many gifts of grace that come our way. And we won't forget to notice when God answers our prayers.

Evening
Life

The Fear-of-GOD expands your life.
PROVERBS 10:27 MSG

People seem hungry for something to give their lives meaning. If you listen to current hit songs, you'd think that meaning comes from having another human being love you more than anyone else in the world. But what happens when that love interest gets mad, disappoints you, or finds someone else? Life becomes a drag. Only developing a relationship with God through Jesus Christ will fill that hole in your heart. Let Him give your life fresh meaning.

MORNING
Not Withholding

Anything I wanted, I would take. I denied myself no pleasure.
I even found great pleasure in hard work, a reward for all my labors.
ECCLESIASTES 2:10 NLT

Work beckons. Deadlines loom. You're trying to balance your home life against your work life, and it's overwhelming. Take heart! It is possible to rejoice in your labors to find pleasure in the day-to-day tasks. At work or at play. . .let the Lord cause a song of joy to rise up in your heart.

EVENING
Building God's Kingdom

And I have filled him with the Spirit of God, in wisdom
and ability, in understanding and intelligence, and in
knowledge, and in all kinds of craftsmanship.
EXODUS 31:3 AMP

Your abilities, your intelligence, your knowledge, and your talents are all gifts of grace from God's generous Spirit. But without wisdom, the ability to see into the spiritual world, none of these gifts is worth very much. Wisdom is what fits together all of the other pieces, allowing us to use our talents to build God's spiritual kingdom.

MORNING
Not Suzie Homemaker

The Spirit has given each of us a special way of serving others.
1 CORINTHIANS 12:7 CEV

My friend Denise has the gift of hospitality. She welcomes people into her home and makes them feel loved through her thoughtful accents: serving food on her best china, lighting scented candles, offering cozy furnishings. Hospitality is not my gift. My guests get bagged chips, flat soda, and leave coated in cat hair. God taught me not to compare and despair, for He has given each of us our *own* gift to be used for His service. What's yours?

EVENING
I'm No Eeyore

Then [Job's] wife said to him, "Do you still hold fast your integrity? Curse God and die!"
JOB 2:9 NASB

Job's wife was the unwilling recipient of Satan's attacks because of her husband's righteous life. When the going got tough, our girl lost faith and hope disintegrated. We, too, sometimes lose sight of all God has done for us and focus only on what He *didn't* do. Our attitudes nosedive and negativity imprisons us. Job's response is the key to escaping the shackles of Eeyore-ism: "I *know* that my Redeemer lives" (Job 19:25 NASB).

MORNING
The Center of Our Lives

*The apostles often met together and prayed
with a single purpose in mind.*
ACTS 1:14 CEV

What do you do when you get together with the people you're close to?
You probably talk and laugh, share a meal, maybe go shopping or work on a
project. But do you ever pray together? If prayer is the center of our lives,
we will want to share this gift of grace with those with whom we're closest.

EVENING
A Glad Heart

*A happy heart makes the face cheerful,
but heartache crushes the spirit.*
PROVERBS 15:13 NIV

Have you ever been so disappointed, so broken down, that you felt you
couldn't go on? Don't despair! Even in the hardest of times, it's possible
to have a glad heart. The body reacts to the spirit, so if you want to
keep on keepin' on, better do a heart check! No doubt, the cheerful
expression on your face is sure to make others ask, "What's her secret?"

MORNING

Joyous Petitions

*Take delight in the LORD, and he
will give you the desires of your heart.*
PSALM 37:4 NIV

What are the deepest desires of your heart? Ponder that question a moment. If you could really do or have what you longed for, what would that be? The key to receiving from the Lord is delighting in Him. Draw near. Spend time with your head against His shoulder, feeling His heartbeat. Ask that your requests come into alignment with His will. Then, with utmost joy, make your petitions known.

EVENING

Listening

To answer before listening—that is folly and shame.
PROVERBS 18:13 NIV

How do you feel when someone listens to you without telling you what to do? Research indicates that this type of interaction helps people find their own answers and take intentional action. Most women (men and children, too) long to be heard and understood. Yet, it's difficult to hear another's bewilderment, pain, *or* joy when you interject your own thoughts and opinions. You may long to provide solutions, but it's wise to listen to the whole story before giving advice. Listening encourages mutual growth.

MORNING
Superwoman Isn't Home

*But we will devote ourselves to
prayer and to the ministry of the word.*
ACTS 6:4 NASB

As busy women, we've found out the hard way that we can't do
everything. Heaven knows we've tried, but the truth has found us out:
superwoman is a myth. So we must make priorities and focus on the
most important. Prayer and God's Word should be our faith priorities. If
we only do as much as we *can* do, then God will take over and do what
only He can do. He's got our backs, girls!

EVENING
Nothing More Valuable

*Wisdom is more valuable than gold and crystal.
It cannot be purchased with jewels mounted in fine gold.*
JOB 28:17 NLT

Money can't buy you love—and it can't buy wisdom either. Wisdom
is more precious than anything this world has to offer. In fact, some
passages of the Old Testament seem to indicate that Wisdom is another
name for Jesus. Just as Jesus is the Way, the Truth, and the Light, He is
also the One who gives us the vision to see God's world all around us.
No other gift is more valuable than Jesus.

MORNING
Alone Time with God

But Jesus often withdrew to the wilderness for prayer.
LUKE 5:16 NLT

God is always with us, even when we're too busy to do more than
whisper a prayer in the shower or as we drive the car. But if even
Jesus needed to make time to get away by Himself for some alone
time with God, then we certainly need to do so, too. In those quiet
moments of prayer, by ourselves with God, we will find the
grace we need to live our busy lives.

EVENING
Confounded Corsets

Cultivate inner beauty, the gentle,
gracious kind that God delights in.
1 PETER 3:4 MSG

In our quest for beauty, we buy into all sorts of crazy things:
mud facials, cosmetic surgery, body piercings, obsessive dieting,
squeezing size 10 feet into size 8 shoes. The image of Scarlett O'Hara's
binding corset makes us shudder. (Reminds me of a pair of jeans I
wrestled with just last week.) Yet God's idea of beauty is on the *inside*—
where spandex cannot touch. Let's resolve to devote more time
pursuing inner beauty that will never require Botox.

MORNING
Working Out

I will never give up hope or stop praising you.
PSALM 71:14 CEV

Praise is like a muscle; if we don't exercise it regularly, it becomes weak and atrophied. But if we flex and extend an attitude of gratitude daily, praise grows into a strong, dependable force that nurtures hope and carries us through the worst of circumstances. Like Helen Keller, though blind and deaf, we'll praise our Creator: "I thank God for my handicaps, for through them, I have found myself, my work, and my God."

EVENING
Rejoice. . .It's Worth Repeating!

Rejoice in the Lord always; again I will say, rejoice!
PHILIPPIANS 4:4 NASB

Have you ever had to repeat yourself to a child, a spouse, or a coworker? When we want to get our point across or think someone's not listening as he or she should we repeat our words. God knows what it's like! Some things are worth repeating, just because they're so good! "Rejoice in the Lord always. . .and again I say, rejoice!" He tells us not just once, but twice. Better listen up!

MORNING
The Fork in the Road

*What do people get for all the toil and anxious
striving with which they labor under the sun?*
ECCLESIASTES 2:22 NIV

Imagine you're approaching a fork in the road. You're unsure of which
way to turn. If you knew ahead of time that the road to the right would
be filled with joy and the road to the left would lead to sorrow, wouldn't
it make the decision easier? Today, as you face multiple decisions, ask
God to lead you down the right road.

EVENING
Options

The soul of the diligent is richly supplied.
PROVERBS 13:4 ESV

I have no choice in the matter. Perhaps you've uttered these words
when facing a difficult decision. If so, you've probably felt the trapped
sensation that accompanies this misbelief. The truth is you *do* have
choices. You can ask questions, research your options, consider the pros
and cons, and then make a reasonable choice based on the knowledge
you have at the time. By your own diligent action, that boxed-in
feeling will subside and you'll enjoy new freedom.

Scripture Index